THE ORIGINS OF SEGREGATION

Problems in American Civilization

The ORIGINS *Of* SEGREGATION

EDITED WITH AN INTRODUCTION BY

Joel Williamson

UNIVERSITY OF NORTH CAROLINA

D. C. HEATH AND COMPANY
A Division of Raytheon Education Company
Lexington, Massachusetts

INTRODUCTION

ONE AUTUMN evening in 1830, Thomas Dartmouth Rice appeared on the stage of the Fifth Street Theater in Pittsburgh, Pennsylvania. At twenty-five, Rice had gained a modest reputation as an actor in the small theaters of the Ohio Valley. But he was better known, and perhaps more appreciated, in the gentlemen's bars along his circuit as an impromptu raconteur, singer, and dancer. On this night, Rice was inspired to test a new act, one which would employ his talent for light entertainment. He had blackened his face to achieve the look of a comic Negro, and he was "habited in an old coat forlornly dilapidated, with a pair of shoes composed equally of patches and places for patches on his feet, and wearing a coarse straw hat in a melancholy condition of rent and collapse over a dense black wig of matted moss . . ." As he shuffled upstage, the usual crunching of peanuts in the pit ceased, and "through the circles passed a murmur and a bustle of liveliest expectation." The orchestra played a short introduction and Rice began to sing and, one imagines, at the same time to wheel, turn, and jump to punctuate the first lines of his song:

O, Jim Crow's come to town, as you all must know
An' he wheel about, he turn about, he do jis so,
An' every time he wheel about he jump Jim Crow.

The delight of the audience was immediate. As Jim Crow continued to sing, contriving lyrics which played upon incidents familiar in Pittsburgh, their laughter and applause expanded. Shortly, the clamor drowned the voice of the comedian and the show, literally a riotous success, had to be closed for the evening.[1]

Thus T. D. ("Daddy") Rice (along with Dan Emmett and E. P. Christy) became a pioneer among Negro minstrels, and "Jim Crow" survived as a label for one stereotype of the American Negro. In the term "Jim Crow laws" it has received a prolonged longevity.

In the middle of the twentieth century most scholars as well as most laymen were ignorant of the origins of segregation and the mass of Jim Crow legislation which was woven into the fabric of race relations. Most Americans probably assumed that segregation had always been with us and that the legislative pattern had developed immediately after Reconstruction. The single most influential work in challenging these assumptions has been C. Vann Woodward's *The Strange Career of Jim Crow*. Professor Woodward, a native of Vanndale, Arkansas, a graduate of Emory University and the University of North Carolina, for many years a professor at the Johns Hopkins University in Baltimore, and a leading historian of the South, is a Southerner with impeccable credentials. Early in the fall of 1954, during the critical lull between the key desegregation decision of the Supreme Court and the rise of "massive resistance" in the South, Professor Woodward gave the James W. Richard Lectures in History to an integrated audience in the University of Virginia. The subject he chose was, appropriately, the strange career of Jim Crow. The history of Jim Crow legislation was strange

[1] Robert Peebles Nevin, "Stephen C. Foster and Negro Minstrelsy," *The Atlantic Monthly*, November 1867, pp. 608–10.

in that it did not come with Redemption but, as he amply illustrated, in the 1890's and afterward. Even more striking and important was Professor Woodward's thesis that the proscription, segregation, and disfranchisement of Negroes were made total and rigid only by this legislation, and that prior to this time race relations were relatively fluid. In presenting his case Professor Woodward drew heavily upon his own previous research in the post-Reconstruction period, particularly those portions of his labor which had been published in *Tom Watson: Agrarian Rebel* (1938) and *Origins of the New South, 1877–1913* (1951). In addition, he cited as especially useful Vernon Lane Wharton's *The Negro in Mississippi, 1865–1890* (1947) and George Brown Tindall's *South Carolina Negroes, 1877–1900* (1952).

A number of monographs relating to the Negro and race relations in each of several Southern states have led to pointed disagreement with that portion of the Woodward thesis which argues for the relatively late genesis of segregation. It is manifestly true that the modern pattern of segregating and discriminating *legislation* came in the last decade of the nineteenth century and subsequently. These laws sometimes instigated segregation in the sense that they applied old attitudes to novel physical situations (as with taxicabs, elevators, and telephone booths). It is also true that integration of a kind did occur before the 1890's, when some Negroes occasionally did exercise their legal right to use public facilities along with whites. Nevertheless, these studies contend that *de facto* segregation of a highly rigid order was widespread soon after emancipation and continued substantially unchanged throughout the period of Reconstruction, despite strenuous counterattacks

launched under the protection of Union occupation forces in the South, Southern Republican legislatures, and the federal Civil Rights Act of 1875. Pertinent evidence is found in Wharton's sections on the Jim Crow laws and miscegenation in Mississippi, in Charles E. Wynes' treatment of "Social Acceptance and Unacceptance" in *Race Relations in Virginia, 1870–1902* (1961), and in the chapter on the separation of the races from *After Slavery: The Negro in South Carolina During Reconstruction, 1861–1877* (1965).

Much more important than the establishment of the time period in which rigid segregation came to be is the ultimate question of its roots. Why did segregation occur? All agree that the phenomenon took place before a backdrop of racial prejudice. Professor Woodward's innovation is that he brought forth a concise and immediate explanation of the event. He did this most clearly at first in the selection from *Origins of the New South, 1877–1913* (1951) which appears below under the title "Why Negroes Were Segregated in the New South." Four years later he elaborated brilliantly upon that theme in *The Strange Career of Jim Crow*, in a chapter which he called "Capitulation to Racism."

In the Woodward thesis, much of the thrust for legal segregation came from the hatred of the Negro felt by lower-class whites, and much of the resistance to racial discrimination from the paternalistic impulse of patricians. In 1961 Professor Charles E. Wynes, publishing the results of his work on race relations in Virginia, concluded that the essential impetus for segregative legislation came from upper-class journalists and politicians and thus offered a significant revision of the Woodward explanation.

Other writers, describing a relatively rigid state of segregation early in Reconstruction, interpreted the separation of the races as a logical outgrowth of racial attitudes held by both Negroes and whites. These attitudes, in turn, are described as the direct legacy of slavery and the philosophical framework that gave it support. There is much evidence in literature of the postwar period to maintain that contention.

Negroes themselves revealed an inclination to withdraw from association with whites once emancipation gave them that opportunity. This was most evident in the churches, but it was also obvious in the schools and in the dissolution of the plantation system. Delegates to the Constitutional Convention of 1868 in South Carolina, an all-Republican body with a Negro majority, recognized a tendency among Negroes and whites to withdraw physically from each other, and in establishing a system of public education they were careful to accommodate these preferences. Francis L. Cardozo, chairman of the committee on education, himself a Negro and principal of the leading Negro school in Charleston, assured the delegates that Negroes would generally prefer separate facilities. He implied that most Negroes would prefer separation to an association which involved painful discrimination.

A radical of another color was Hinton Rowan Helper, a North Carolinian whose book *The Impending Crisis of the South* (1857) had created such a furor before secession. This volume had called upon the yeomen farmers of the South to rise against slavery. After the war, still a vociferous, if self-appointed, spokesman for the common man of the South, Helper demanded the total exclusion of the Negro from the white man's civilization. At the other end of the social scale, and representative of conservative patricians, was Dr. James R. Sparkman, a low-country South Carolina rice planter, physician, and aristocrat in the "Bourbon" style. Writing an essay on "The Negro" about 1889, Dr. Sparkman, who was neither a politician nor a journalist with a professional mission to perform, revealed the thinking of one paternalist on the Negro problem.

George Washington Cable, a native of Louisiana and a writer of national prominence, was a Southern patrician with a strong humanitarian bent. In 1885, in an article entitled "The Silent South," he depicted a rigid color line in most areas of interracial relationships. Addressing himself directly to the question of why such conditions prevailed, he concluded that it was because some gentlemen had made the mistake of confusing civil rights for the Negro with social equality and the danger of racial amalgamation. They made the mistake quite naturally, he maintained, because they labored still under racial attitudes fixed by the circumstances of slavery.

The writers cited above attempted to explain the when and why of segregation in the South after the Civil War. Other authors have added new and vital dimensions to our understanding of the problem. Professor Richard C. Wade, in a close study of slavery in several Southern cities, pressed the beginning of segregation back into the prewar South and explained its appearance in an essentially new interpretation. Leon F. Litwack, in *North of Slavery* (1961), not only described a thorough pattern of segregation extant in the North in the prewar period, but attributed it to a pervasive spirit of racial prejudice. Finally, Mr. Benjamin H. Hunt, a contemporary writing about Philadelphia in 1865 and 1866, depicted graphically the high degree of segregation which persisted in this key Northern city and attempted to make clear its cause.

Our materials bristle with questions: What is meant by "segregation?" Does the term connote a mental as well as a physical rejection of one race by another? What is meant by "integration," "desegregation," "discrimination," "civil equality," "public equality," and "social equality?"

Did segregation become rigid in the 1890's and afterward, or during Reconstruction? Or, indeed, was the basic pattern set in the South or the North even before emancipation? Before the 1890's, precisely how much integration (rather than segregation) was there? Did the Jim Crow laws of the 1890's and afterward "substantially" alter the nature of segregation, or did they merely state what already existed in substance? Was there a difference between segregation in the older Southern states of the East and the newer states of the West? Was there a difference between rural and urban areas in attitudes toward Negroes?

On the other side, are the indications of early de facto segregation in South Carolina, Virginia, and Mississippi valid proof that rigid segregation existed in those states soon after emancipation? Particularly, does either Wynes' or Wharton's evidence support an argument for or against an early pattern of rigid segregation? Even if one accepts the existence of early and firm segregation in South Carolina, Virginia, and Mississippi, can he generalize that the same held true for the whole South?

All agree that a comprehensive color line had been established in the South before about 1913. Define that line as precisely as you can by describing the racial pattern in public and private places. Then consider the very important question of why segregation came to be. Were the Jim Crow laws the fruit of frustration? Or were they enacted because the apathy of the North and the political impotence of the Negro in the South made it safe to do so? Was segregation itself caused by the frustrations of the 1890's; was it, after all, the result of a chance combination of events, almost a case of mistaken identity in which the Negro was substituted for the ills bred of rapid and rampant industrialization? Were racial attitudes and race relations truly malleable in the 1880's and early 1890's; did the attitudes of Southern conservatives, Northern liberals, and Southern radicals offer possible alternatives to the racism of the early twentieth century? Was there a significant difference in the attitude of Southern conservatives toward Negroes which produced a substantive difference in their behavior toward them; were the attitudes and actions of patricians different from those of the small farmer, the "cracker," the "red neck," and the "poor white"? Were Southern white attitudes and actions different from those of the North? Would the continued support of the Negro's rights by the North have prevented his segregation and degradation? Did the North change its mind about the Negro in 1877, or 1890, or at all? How real was the possibility that Southern radicals would ally themselves with Negroes? If real, what were the bases of that alliance? Was there a possibility that such an alliance could secure, in addition to political and economic advantages, "public equality" for the Negro? Were the Southern radicals in any sense pro-Negro? Were they potentially pro-Negro? How important was Southern white fear of racial intermixture in creating and maintaining segregation? What was the answer of the liberals to this fear? Did Negroes withdraw from contact with whites to such an extent as significantly to promote segregation? Where, when, and why did they withdraw? Can we conclude that Negroes really *wanted* segregation? Assuming that the great mass of whites believed Negroes to be innately inferior to Caucasians, is the case really proved that segregation springs out of basic attitudes on race held by both Negroes and whites? For instance, could not segregation be better accounted for by reference primarily to economic and political forces?

Was the segregation that Professor Wade described in the antebellum period the same in form and causation as that which followed emancipation? Was it the progenitor of the modern pattern? Was segregation in the North significantly different from that in the South either in form or motivation? Did Southerners, in brief, learn segregation from the North?

Echoes of these troublesome questions still live with us today. Professor Robin Williams, speaking with the authority which social science has earned by a century of labor, reminds us of the timelessness and universality of the problem of establishing meaningful relationships with our neighbors of different ethnic origins. Using the materials here presented, what answers can you offer to the problem of race relations with which we are now confronted?

CONTENTS

The Clash of Issues

Historians are not in agreement on the time when segregation in the South became rigid. C. Vann Woodward and George Brown Tindall describe segregation as occurring only in the 1890's and afterward:

> After Redemption was achieved the new governments of the Southern states retained such segregation practices as had been established during or before Reconstruction, but showed little immediate disposition to expand the code into new fields. Much less was there evidence of a movement to make segregation universal, such as it was to become in the twentieth century.
>
> C. Vann Woodward

> At the end of the Reconstruction period the pattern of racial segregation had not been rigidly defined.
>
> George Brown Tindall

Another historian describes it as a Reconstruction phenomenon:

> By the end of Reconstruction, Negroes had won the legal right to enjoy, along with whites, accommodations in all public places. In reality, however, they seldom did so. On the opposite side of the racial frontier, the pattern of separation was fixed in the minds of the whites almost simultaneously with the emancipation of the Negro. By 1868, the physical color line had, for the most part, already crystallized.
>
> Joel Williamson

Authorities also disagree as to the causes of segregation. One eminent historian relates discrimination to the popularization of government in the South about the turn of the century:

> The barriers of racial discrimination mounted in direct ratio with the tide of political democracy among whites. In fact, an increase of Jim Crow laws upon the statute books of a state is almost an accurate index of the decline of the reactionary regimes of the Redeemers and triumph of white democratic movements.
>
> C. Vann Woodward

Whereas in 1868 a Southern white saw segregation as the result of a natural instinct of race:

> There are many points of general dissatisfaction and dispute, which should not, on any account, be overlooked in the discussion of the subjects here presented. One of these is, that white people, whose reason and honor have not been vitiated, object to close

relationship with negroes, not wishing to live with them in the same house; not wishing to fellowship with them in the same society, assembly, or congregation; not wishing to ride with them in the same omnibus, car, or carriage; and not wishing to mess with them at the same table, whether at a hotel, in a restaurant, on a steamer, or elsewhere.

HINTON ROWAN HELPER

Other historians have added new dimensions to the problem. Richard C. Wade pushes the beginnings of segregation back into the period of slavery and advances a totally novel explanation of its origins:

As the institution of slavery encountered mounting difficulties, and as its control over the blacks weakened, another arrangement was devised which maintained great social distance within the physical proximity of town life. Increasingly public policy tried to separate the races whenever the surveillance of the master was likely to be missing. To do this, the distinction between slave and free Negro was erased; race became more important than legal status; and a pattern of segregation emerged inside the broader framework of the "peculiar institution."

RICHARD C. WADE

And still another historian sees segregation fully established in the North well before the period with which Professor Wade is concerned:

In virtually every phase of existence, Negroes found themselves systematically separated from whites. They were either excluded from railway cars, omnibuses, stagecoaches, and steamboats or assigned to special "Jim Crow" sections; they sat, when permitted, in secluded and remote corners of theaters and lecture halls; they could not enter most hotels, restaurants, and resorts, except as servants; they prayed in "Negro pews" in the white churches, and if partaking of the sacrament of the Lord's Supper, they waited until the whites had been served the bread and wine. Moreover, they were often educated in segregated schools, punished in segregated prisons, nursed in segregated hospitals, and buried in segregated cemeteries. . . . To most northerners, segregation constituted not a departure from democratic principles, as certain foreign critics alleged, but simply the working out of natural laws, the inevitable consequence of the racial inferiority of the Negro.

LEON F. LITWACK

I. THE GENESIS OF SEGREGATION

C. Vann Woodward: THE STRANGE CAREER OF JIM CROW

In the fall of 1954 Professor C. Vann Woodward delivered the James W. Richard Lectures at the University of Virginia. In those lectures Professor Woodward, preeminent as an authority on postbellum Southern history, suggested that race relations in the South had not always been what Southerners assumed them to be; that indeed Jim Crow had had an astoundingly strange career. Coming in the wake of the Supreme Court decision on segregation in the public schools and while the South was still defining its response, the lectures were deeply appropriate to the times. Early in 1955 they were printed by the Oxford University Press and achieved a wide and immediate success. Soon, The Strange Career of Jim Crow joined Gunnar Myrdal's An American Dilemma (1944)* as one of the two most frequently cited works on Negro-white relations in the United States, it will long endure as a model of excellence in the writing of purposive history. Dr. Woodward is Sterling Professor of History at Yale University.

IN THE first place it is necessary to clear away some prevailing misconceptions about this latest of lost causes. One of them grows out of a tendency to identify and confuse it with an earlier lost cause. The assumption is often made that Reconstruction constituted an interruption of normal relations between the races in the South. Once the carpetbaggers were overthrown and "Home Rule" was established, the founding fathers of the New South, after conceding that slavery was finished and the Negro was now a freedman and more vaguely a citizen, are presumed to have restored to normality the disturbed relations between whites

and blacks. To conceive of the new order of race relations as a restoration, however, is to forget the nature of relations between races under the old regime. For one thing segregation would have been impractical under slavery, and for another the circumstances that later gave rise to the segregation code did not exist so long as the Negro was enslaved. "Before and directly after the war," writes W. E. B. Du Bois, "when all the best of the Negroes were domestic servants in the best of the white families, there were bonds of intimacy, affection, and sometimes blood relationship, between the races. They lived in the same home, shared in the family life, often attended the same church, and talked and conversed with each other." These condi-

* Gunnar Myrdal, *An American Dilemma* (2 vols., New York: Harper & Row, 1944).

tions could certainly not be said to have been "restored'" by segregation.

A second misconception is more common and is shared by a number of historians. While recognizing that the new order was new and not the restoration of an old system, they sometimes make the assumption that it followed automatically upon the overthrow of Reconstruction as an immediate consequence of Redemption. Those who cherish the new order of segregation, Jim Crowism, and disfranchisement, therefore, often attribute it to the Redeemers, the founding fathers of the New South. Their defense of the system clothes it with the moral prestige they attribute to Redemption, and their indignation against any attack upon it is fired by the zeal of the historic struggle for home rule and the emotional heritage of the Civil War period. Their identification of the two causes is understandable but unjustified, and it lingers to complicate and confuse adjustment to the New Reconstruction.

As a matter of fact, some important aspects of segregation were achieved and sanctioned by the First Reconstruction. One of these was segregation of the great Protestant churches, a process accomplished by the voluntary withdrawal of the Negroes and their establishment of independent organizations of their own. Whatever the intentions of the framers of the Fourteenth Amendment were regarding segregation in the public schools — a controversy that even the Supreme Court in its historic decision of 17 May 1954 declined to settle — the fact is that segregation became the almost universal practice in the public schools of the South during Reconstruction, with or without explicit sanction of the radicals. In a third important field, the military services, segregation was strengthened by

the Civil War and left unaltered during Reconstruction. As for equality in social gatherings of a private nature, there is little evidence that even the high Negro officials of Reconstruction governments in the South were extended that recognition — even by the white radicals.

After Redemption was achieved the new governments of the Southern states retained such segregation practices as had been established during or before Reconstruction, but showed little immediate disposition to expand the code into new fields. Much less was there evidence of a movement to make segregation universal, such as it was to become in the twentieth century. More than a decade was to pass after Redemption before the first Jim Crow law was to appear upon the law books of a Southern state, and more than two decades before the older states of Virginia, North Carolina, and South Carolina were to adopt such laws.

Suspicions of the South's intentions toward the freedmen after the withdrawal of federal troops were naturally rife in the North. In 1878 Colonel Thomas Wentworth Higginson went south to investigate for himself. The report of his findings, published in *The Atlantic Monthly,* is of particular interest in view of the Colonel's background. One of the most militant abolitionists, Higginson had been one of the "Secret Six" who conspired with John Brown before the Harpers Ferry raid, and during the war he had organized and led a combat regiment of Negro troops. In Virginia, South Carolina, and Florida, the states he visited in 1878, he found "a condition of outward peace" and wondered immediately if there did not lurk beneath it "some covert plan for crushing or reenslaving the colored race." If so, he decided, it would "show itself in some personal ill usage of the blacks, in the withdrawal of privileges, in legislation endangering their rights." But, he reported, "I can assert that, carrying with me the eyes of a tolerably suspicious abolitionist, I saw none of these indications." He had expected to be affronted by contemptuous or abusive treatment of Negroes. "During this trip," however, he wrote, "I had absolutely no occasion for any such attitude." Nor was this due to "any cringing demeanor on the part of the blacks, for they show much more manhood than they once did." He compared the tolerance and acceptance of the Negro in the South on trains and street cars, at the polls, in the courts and legislatures, in the police force and militia, with attitudes in his native New England and decided that the South came off rather better in the comparison. "How can we ask more of the States formerly in rebellion," he demanded, "than that they should be abreast of New England in granting rights and privileges to the colored race? Yet this is now the case in the three states I name; or at least if they fall behind in some points, they lead at some points." Six years later, in a review of the situation in the South, Higginson found no reason to change his estimate of 1878.

The year 1879 provides testimony to the point from a foreign observer. Sir George Campbell, a member of Parliament, traveled over a large part of the South, with race relations as the focus of his interest. He was impressed with the freedom of association between whites and blacks, with the frequency and intimacy of personal contact, and with the extent of Negro participation in political affairs. He commented with particular surprise on the equality with which Negroes shared public facilities. He remarked that "the humblest black rides with the proudest white on terms of perfect equality, and without the smallest symptom of malice or dislike on either side. I was, I confess, surprised to see how completely this is the case; even an English Radical is a little taken aback at first."

In the first year of Redemption a writer who signed himself "A South Carolinian" in *The Atlantic Monthly* corroborated the observations of the Englishman regarding the Negro's equality of treatment on common carriers, trains, and street cars. "The negroes are freely admitted to the theatre in Columbia and to other exhibitions, lectures, etc.," though the whites avoided sitting with them "if the hall be not crowded," he added. "In Columbia they are also served at the bars, soda water fountains, and ice-cream saloons, but not generally elsewhere."

Twenty years later, in 1897, a Charleston editor referring to a proposed Jim Crow law for trains wrote: "We care nothing whatever about Northern or outside opinion in this matter. It is a question for our own decision according to our own ideas of what is right and expedient. And our opinion is that we have no more need for a Jim Crow system this year than we had last year, and a great deal less than we had twenty and thirty years ago." In his view such a law was "unnecessary and uncalled for," and furthermore it would be "a needless affront to our respectable and well behaved colored people."

Southern white testimony on the subject has naturally been discounted as propaganda. If only by way of contrast with later views, however, the following editorial from the Richmond *Dispatch*, 13 October 1886, is worth quoting: "Our State Constitution requires all State officers in their oath of office to declare that they 'recognize and accept the civil and political equality of all men.' We repeat that nobody here objects to sitting in political conventions with negroes. Nobody here objects to serving on juries with negroes. No lawyer objects to practicing law in court where negro lawyers practice . . . Colored men are allowed to introduce bills into the Virginia Legislature; and in both branches of this body negroes are allowed to sit, as they have a right to sit." George Washington Cable, the aggressive agitator for the rights of Negroes, protested strongly against discrimination elsewhere, but is authority for the statement made in 1885, that "In Virginia they may ride exactly as white people do and in the same cars."

More pertinent and persuasive is the testimony of the Negro himself. In April 1885, T. McCants Stewart set forth from Boston to visit his native state of South Carolina after an absence of ten years. A Negro newspaperman, corresponding editor of the New York *Freeman*, Stewart was conscious of his role as a spokesman and radical champion of his race. "On leaving Washington, D.C.," he reported to his paper, "I put a chip on my shoulder, and inwardly dared any man to knock it off." He found a seat in a car which became so crowded that several white passengers had to sit on their baggage. "I fairly foamed at the mouth," he wrote, "imagining that the conductor would order me into a seat occupied by a colored lady so as to make room for a white passenger." Nothing of the sort happened, however, nor was there any unpleasantness when Stewart complained of a request from a white Virginian that he shift his baggage so that the white man could sit beside him. At a stop twenty-one miles below Petersburg he entered a station dining room, "bold as a lion," he wrote, took a seat at a table with white people, and was courteously served. "The whites at the table appeared not to note my presence," he reported. "Thus far I

had found travelling more pleasant . . . than in some parts of New England." Aboard a steamboat in North Carolina he complained of a colored waiter who seated him at a separate table, though in the same dining room with whites. At Wilmington, however, he suffered from no discrimination in dining arrangements. His treatment in Virginia and North Carolina, he declared, "contrasted strongly with much that I have experienced in dining rooms in the North." Another contrast that impressed him was the ease and frequency with which white people entered into conversation with him for no other purpose than to pass the time of day. "I think the whites of the South," he observed, "are really less afraid to [have] contact with colored people than the whites of the North."

Stewart continued his journey southward rejoicing that "Along the Atlantic seaboard from Canada to the Gulf of Mexico — through Delaware, Maryland, Virginia, the Carolinas, Georgia and into Florida, all the old slave States with enormous Negro populations . . . a first-class ticket is good in a first-class coach; and Mr. [Henry W.] Grady would be compelled to ride with a Negro, or, walk." From Columbia, South Carolina, he wrote: "I feel about as safe here as in Providence, R.I. I can ride in first-class cars on the railroads and in the streets. I can go into saloons and get refreshments even as in New York. I can stop in and drink a glass of soda and be more politely waited upon than in some parts of New England." He also found that "Negroes dine with whites in a railroad saloon" in his native state. He watched a Negro policeman arrest a white man "under circumstances requiring coolness, prompt decision, and courage"; and in Charleston he witnessed the review of hundreds of Negro troops. "Indeed," wrote Stewart, "the Palmetto State leads the South in some things. May she go on advancing in liberal practices and prospering throughout her borders, and may she be like leaven to the South; like a star unto 'The Land of Flowers,' leading our blessed section on and on into the way of liberty, justice, equality, truth, and righteousness."

One significant aspect of Stewart's newspaper reports should be noted. They were written a month after the inauguration of Grover Cleveland and the return of the Democrats to power for the first time in twenty-four years. His paper had opposed Cleveland, and propaganda had been spread among Negro voters that the return of the Democrats would mean the end of freedmen's rights, if not their liberty. Stewart failed to find what he was looking for, and after a few weeks cut his communications short with the comment that he could find "nothing spicy or exciting to write." "For the life of [me]," he confessed, "I can't 'raise a row' in these letters. Things seem (remember I write seem) to move along as smoothly as in New York or Boston . . . If you should ask me 'watchman, tell us of the night' . . . I would say, 'The morning light is breaking.' "

So far nearly all the evidence presented has come from the older states of the eastern seaboard. In writing of slavery under the old regime it is common for historians to draw distinctions between the treatment of slaves in the upper and older South and their lot in the lower South and the newer states. In the former their condition is generally said to have been better than it was in the latter. It is worth remarking an analogous distinction in the treatment of the race in the era of segregation. It is clear at least that the newer states were inclined to resort to Jim Crow laws earlier than the older commonwealths of the seaboard, and there is evidence that segregation and discrimination became generally practiced before they became law. Even so, there are a number of indications that segregation and ostracism were not nearly so harsh and rigid in the early years as they became later.

In his study of conditions in Mississippi, Vernon Wharton reveals that for some years "most of the saloons served whites and Negroes at the same bar. Many of the restaurants, using separate tables, served both races in the same room . . . On May 21, 1879, the Negroes of Jackson, after a parade of their fire company, gave a picnic in Hamilton Park. On the night of May 29, 'the ladies of the [white] Episcopal Church' used Hamilton Park for a *fete*. After their picnic the Negroes went to Angelo's Hall for a dance. This same hall was used for white dances and parties, and was frequently the gathering place of Democratic conventions... Throughout the state common cemeteries, usually in separate portions, held the graves of both whites and Negroes." Wharton points out, however, that as early as 1890 segregation had closed in and the Negroes were by that date excluded from saloons, restaurants, parks, public halls, and white cemeteries.

At the International Exposition in New Orleans in 1885 Charles Dudley Warner watched with some astonishment as "white and colored people mingled freely, talking and looking at what was of common interest . . . On 'Louisiana Day' in the Exposition the colored citizens," he reported, "took their full share of the parade and the honors. Their societies marched with the others, and the races mingled in the grounds in unconscious equality of privileges." While he was in the city he also saw "a colored clergyman in his surplice seated in the chancel of the most important white Episcopal church in New Orleans, assisting the service."

A frequent topic of comment by Northern visitors during the period was the intimacy of contact between the races in the South, an intimacy sometimes admitted to be distasteful to the visitor. Standard topics were the sight of white babies suckled at black breasts, white and colored children playing together, the casual proximity of white and Negro homes in the cities, the camaraderie of maidservant and mistress, employer and employee, customer and clerk, and the usual stories of cohabitation of white men and Negro women. The same sights and stories had once been favorite topics of comment for the carpetbaggers and before them of the abolitionists, both of whom also expressed puzzlement and sometimes revulsion. What the Northern traveler of the eighties sometimes took for signs of a new era of race relations was really a heritage of slavery times, or, more elementally, the results of two peoples having lived together intimately for a long time and learned to like and trust each other — whatever their formal relations were, whether those of master and slave, exploiter and exploited, or superior and inferior.

It would certainly be preposterous to leave the impression that any evidence I have submitted indicates a golden age of race relations in the period between Redemption and segregation. On the contrary, the evidence of race conflict and violence, brutality and exploitation in this very period is overwhelming. It was, after all, in the eighties and early nineties that lynching attained the most staggering proportions ever reached in the history of that crime. Moreover, the fanatical advocates of racism, whose doctrines of total segregation, disfranchisement, and ostracism eventually triumphed over all opposition and became universal practice in the South, were already at work and already beginning to establish dominance over some phases of Southern life. Before their triumph was complete, however, there transpired a period of history whose significance has been hitherto neglected. Exploitation there was in that period, as in other periods and in other regions, but it did not follow then that the exploited had to be ostracized. Subordination there was also, unmistakable subordination; but it was not yet an accepted corollary that the subordinates had to be totally segregated and needlessly humiliated by a thousand daily reminders of their subordination. Conflict there was, too, violent conflict in which the advantage lay with the strong and the dominant, as always; but conflict of some kind was unavoidable short of forceful separation of the races.

George Brown Tindall: THE COLOR LINE

One of the sources upon which Professor Woodward relied most heavily was the following chapter from George Brown Tindall's South Carolina Negroes, 1877–1900. *Professor Tindall is a member of the Department of History in the University of North Carolina, Chapel Hill.*

From George Brown Tindall, *South Carolina Negroes, 1877–1900*, pp. 291–302. Copyright 1952 by the University of South Carolina Press, Columbia. Reprinted by permission. A paperback edition of this volume was issued by the Louisiana State University Press in 1966.

AT THE END of the Reconstruction period the pattern of racial segregation had not been rigidly defined. The public schools were segregated, although some students of the period have misinterpreted a provision in the Constitution of 1868 as requiring mixed schools, and the mixed student body of South Carolina University disbanded in 1877. The two races for the most part attended separate churches. In personal relationships, involving the exercise of individual choice, Negroes and whites had seldom intermingled on a basis of equality. Negroes were seldom admitted to white homes on any basis other than a servile relationship and whites seldom visited Negroes in their homes for any other than business and philanthropic missions. Wherever crowds collected there was a tendency for the two races to gather in groups by themselves.[1]

There was no basis in law for segregation. It was then, as today, enforced largely by social custom. The Supreme Court had not yet discovered the doctrine of "separate, but equal" facilities, and both the federal and state governments, in fact, had statutory prohibitions against segregation on public carriers and in places of public resort. The Republican state legislature had passed such laws in 1869 and 1870. The second and stronger of the two established it as the policy of the state "that no person is entitled to special privileges, or to be preferred before any other person in public matters, but all persons are equal before the law. . . ." It then proceeded to declare that it was unlawful for common carriers, or any person engaged in a business, calling, or pursuit for which a license or charter was required from the federal, state, or mu-

nicipal government, to discriminate between persons on account of race, color, or previous condition. Persons guilty of violating the law were to be fined $1,000 and imprisoned five years, with an additional year if the fine were not paid. Persons in charge of any facility in which the discrimination took place were to be considered as aiding and abetting the offense, and with others who aided and abetted in discrimination, were to be liable to three years' imprisonment, disfranchisement, and disqualification from holding office. In addition, the person or corporation under whose authority the offense should take place was subject to the loss of charter or license.[2]

The law was left on the statute books by the incoming Democratic administration, partly because of the conciliatory Hampton policy but largely because of the fact that it overlapped federal civil rights laws and no particular purpose would be served by its repeal. However, there is no case on record of anyone's ever having been convicted under the law.[3]

When the Supreme Court in 1883 declared provisions of the federal civil rights law of 1875 unconstitutional, Negroes expressed widespread chagrin and protest meetings were held all over the country. In South Carolina, however, the protest was discreetly held to a minimum. "Let us be patient," William Holloway advised his readers. "The objection to our commingling unreservedly with the whites, can be overcome, by education, and by such personal methods as will make us more presentable, than we could possibly be, under the degrading conditions of slavery, in its humanest administration.

---

[1] A South Carolinian, *Atlantic Monthly*, XXXIX (June, 1877), 676.

[2] *Acts and Joint Resolutions* (1869–1870), pp. 386–88.

[3] Charleston *News and Courier*, November 5, 1883.

This cannot be done in a day, or in a year. It will take time. . . ."[4] Sam Lee cautioned the readers of the Charleston *New Era* not to rock the boat since the state of South Carolina had a civil rights law equally as strong as the invalidated federal law.[5] With this admonition Negroes "hauled in their horns, for fear that they might be sawed off at the next Legislature," as one white editor put it.[6] In Columbia an indignation meeting of Negroes was quietly called off after Wade Hampton, in a conversation with Postmaster Wilder, advised against it.[7]

Surprisingly, there was no clamor for the repeal of the state law. The *News and Courier*, in fact, advised its retention.

The Democracy would be untrue to themselves and their pledges, and blind to their own interests, if, by repealing the State Civil Rights law at this time, they gave notice to the world that the law had only been allowed to remain on the Statute books because a United States law covered the same ground, and could be invoked by any persons who were discriminated against.[8]

The state civil rights law was left on the statute books until the end of the eighties. Its demise was made certain by the rise of the Tillman movement, and in 1888 a bill for its repeal was introduced by a young Tillmanite named John Gary Evans. The bill was referred to the Judiciary Committee of the House of Representatives but no action was taken until the following year.[9] In 1889, after several railroads had experimented with "separate but equal accommodations for passengers of the two races" travelling to the State Fair, Governor J. P. Richardson declared in his annual message that the experiment had been successful and that the state civil rights law should be amended so that carriers might be relieved of "disabilities under which they have been placed by those who no longer represent the state." Evans then reintroduced his bill, which passed the lower house without a record vote, but was defeated in the senate by a vote of 15–14. However, strong lobbying apparently pulled it through, for on the following day the senate voted 19–12 for reconsideration. Yet on a final vote, with the bill having been made a strong public issue, there were still four white senators who voted against it, three from Low Country areas of large Negro population and one, surprisingly, from the Up Country county of Laurens.[10] The difficulty in obtaining the repeal of the state civil rights law indicates that white unanimity on the issue of segregation was not complete, or at least that the partisans of Hampton were still willing to go far in the policy of adhering to the pledges of 1876.

During the period of the effectiveness of the law Negroes frequently were admitted to places of public accommodation, not so much because of the law as because of accepted custom. B. O. Townsend noted at the end of the Reconstruction period that in Columbia Negroes were freely admitted to theaters, exhibitions, and lectures, although they were usually given a wide berth by the whites if the hall were not crowded.[11] When the New Orleans Jubilee Singers appeared at Columbia in 1880 to give a performance for the benefit of Howard School, the Opera House, "the resort of the fashion

[4] Charleston *New Era*, October 20, 1883.
[5] *Ibid.*, November 3, 1883.
[6] *Ibid.*, quoting Aiken *Recorder*.
[7] Charleston *News and Courier*, November 5, 1883.
[8] *Ibid.*
[9] *House Journal* (1888), p. 159.

[10] *Ibid.* (1889), pp. 49, 277; *Senate Journal* (1889), pp. 397–98, 416–17.
[11] A South Carolinian, *Atlantic Monthly*, XXXIX (June, 1877), 676.

and elegance of the capital," was filled by an audience of both races.[12] The Charleston *New Era* frequently reviewed performances given at the Charleston Academy of Music, a practice indicating that Negroes were admitted there.[13] As late as 1885, and probably later, there was no formal discrimination in the theaters of Charleston.[14] In the rural areas and smaller towns Negroes did not generally gain admission to such places, but they were almost invariably admitted to circuses, although usually seated in a separate section while the clowns and other performers pointedly faced the whites. Minstrels usually made jokes on Negroes and the Republican party.[15]

In Columbia, at least, Negroes were served at the bars, soda fountains, and ice cream parlors.[16] This was still true as late as 1885, and T. McCants Stewart, who visited Columbia on a reporting mission for the New York *Age* in that year, reported rapturously:

I can ride in first class cars on the railroads and in the streets. I can go into saloons and get refreshments even as in New York. I can stop in and drink a glass of soda and be more politely waited upon than in some parts of New England. Indeed, the Palmetto State leads the South in some things. May she go on advancing in liberal practices and prospering throughout her borders; and may she be like leaven unto the South; like a star

unto 'The Land of Flowers,' leading this our blessed section on and on in the way of liberty, justice, equality, truth and righteousness.[17]

However, Stewart was writing but one year before the inauguration of the farmers' movement by Ben Tillman. The movement, based on racial animosity as well as agrarian discontent, carried Ben Tillman into office as governor in 1890. Tillman's anti-Negro propaganda, which culminated after a decade in the disfranchising convention of 1895, also resulted in the hardening of the color line by the end of the century.

On the other hand, Negroes were invariably excluded from the hotels. The Charleston *News and Courier* explained with masterful evasion that at the hotels "the colored people are not received because their reception would interfere with the accommodation and comfort of the white people — especially of the visitors from the North and West. . . ."[18] In the larger towns Negroes could find accommodations in boarding houses maintained for them.[19]

There was in residential districts during this period no strenuous effort to achieve geographical segregation. A Northern reporter found it curious to notice both in the country and in the city "the proximity and confusion, so to speak, of white and negro houses."[20] In the older districts of coastal towns, such as Charleston and Beaufort, the absence of residential segregation is still noticeable.

In the subtle forms of personal address racial distinctions found frequent expression. Negroes were expected to address

[12] Columbia *Daily Register*, March 8, 1880.
[13] For example: "The opera *Il Trovatore*, which was so superbly rendered by amateurs at the Academy of Music, will be repeated by request, next Tuesday evening." Charleston *New Era*, November 24, 1883.
[14] Charleston *News and Courier*, April 3, 1885. A Negro citizen of Charleston recalled that he was admitted to the Academy of Music without segregation until after the turn of the century. Conversation with Dr. J. A. McFall, July, 1951.
[15] A South Carolinian, *Atlantic Monthly*, XXXIX (June, 1877), 676, 681.
[16] *Ibid.*, p. 676.

[17] New York *Age*, April 25, 1885.
[18] Charleston *News and Courier*, April 3, 1885.
[19] A South Carolinian, *Atlantic Monthly*, XXXIX (June, 1877), 676.
[20] Hogan, *International Review*, VIII (February, 1880), pp. 105–19.

whites as Massa, Master, Boss, Miss, or Missis. The use of Mr. or Mrs. in addressing a white was by many considered an impertinence. Whites generally addressed Negroes by their first names, except the elderly ones, who were addressed as uncle, daddy, aunty, or mauma. It was extremely rare for whites to use Mr. before the name of a Negro except where they needed his vote in the legislature or had some other favor to seek. In formal relationships, however, Negro leaders or officeholders were given the courtesy title and newspapers occasionally referred to the leaders of the race as "Mr.," although they usually tried to avoid it by using some other title, as "Senator," "Sheriff," "Colonel," or "Professor."[21] As late as 1900 the practice had not faded, and the *News and Courier* referred to Booker T. Washington as "Mr. Washington."[22] Capitalization of the proper noun "Negro," a minor point of grammar that has since assumed major proportions as a symbol of attitudes, never became an issue during the period. Whites and Negroes alike wrote the word with an uncapitalized "n." Only one white paper, the Yorkville *Enquirer*, adopted the practice of capitalization, stating that it did so out of deference to the decision of a group of Negroes who had met in Memphis, Tennessee, in the early nineties, and after canvassing various terms for the race, as "nigger," "Afro-American," "colored man," and "freedman," had finally settled on the term "Negro."[23]

The question of miscegenation always created the most tense issue of race relations where the intimacy involved a Negro man and a white woman. Under the system of slavery there had some-times been a degree of intimacy between the plantation owner, his sons, and the overseers and the female slaves. It was through relationships of this kind that the greater portion of the mulatto population came into existence. After freedom such relationships continued, but in a less favorable atmosphere for their perpetuation. Nevertheless, relationships of this kind had never come into conflict with the widespread white fear of "amalgamation," since the children of such relationships followed the race of the mother and became Negroes.

The intimacies of white women with Negro men seem to have been rare, but some such cases, because they were unusual and because they attracted almost unanimous white disapproval, were more forcefully brought to the public eye. When legislation was introduced in the Democratic legislature of 1879 to outlaw interracial marriage, one of the most telling arguments in its favor was the statement by a member from York County that in Fort Mill township, where he resided, there were at least twenty-five or thirty white women living with colored men as husbands, most of them having come from North Carolina which already had a law against interracial marriage.[24] There was, on the other hand, a surprising amount of opposition to the measure. One white Democrat held it to be "impolitic, unnecessary, unwise and unconstitutional both under the Federal and State constitution";[25] another argued that because of religious scruples he deemed it "preferable that our people should enter the marriage relation rather than live in concupiscence."[26] Negro members adopted the argument that the measure

[21] A South Carolinian, *Atlantic Monthly*, XXXIX (June, 1877), 675–76.
[22] Charleston *News and Courier*, July 19, 1900.
[23] Yorkville *Enquirer*, September 6, 1893.

[24] Columbia *Daily Register*, December 4, 1879.
[25] *Ibid.*
[26] *Ibid.*, December 10, 1879.

interfered with individual liberty, and a Negro Democrat from Charleston argued,

The prevention of the intermarriage of the races is not a political issue. This is a social question, which is regulated by the parties themselves. I object to this bill only on the ground that it is striking at the liberty of the colored man, while it is an indirect assault upon the white man's rights. Each individual has the right to choose his own companion. Efforts have been made to show that intermarriages injuriously affect the white race. You have so effectually held yourselves together in the past, that there seems but little propect of our race affecting the white race now. This legislation is wholly unnecessary.[27]

The legislature, however, passed the bill making it "unlawful for any white man to intermarry with any woman of either the Indian or negro races, or any mulatto, mestizoe or half breed, or for any white woman to intermarry with any person other than a white man, or for any mulatto, half breed, negro, Indian or mestizoe to intermarry with a white woman." Persons who violated the act were guilty of a misdemeanor and subject to a fine of not less than $500 or imprisonment for not less than twelve months. The person who performed a marriage ceremony in violation of the act was subject to a like penalty.[28]

A Northern reporter who observed the action of the legislature could not see the objective as anything other than political, "as legitimate miscegenation has never been a habit in South Carolina."[29] It would seem that his interpretation of the measure as chiefly political in motivation was correct; certainly, only few cases can be found of its application. A white

woman charged with marrying a Negro in Kershaw County pleaded guilty in 1881 and was sentenced to twelve months in the county jail.[30] In York the same year a white woman and Negro man were convicted of living unlawfully in wedlock. The woman insisted that her family was generally regarded as being of mixed blood, but the presiding judge in the case charged the jury to decide all doubt as to her white ancestry "in her favor." It was so decided, and she was found guilty.[31] A white man of Union County was sentenced in 1882, although he pleaded in palliation of his case that he had married the Negro woman in question while drunk and had deserted her as soon as he became sober.[32]

Despite the law against interracial marriage there seems to have been no action taken against the illegitimate relationships of white men and Negro women. The Columbia *Daily Register* in 1879 complained of the "white male adulterers who more or less infest every community in our State," and urged that "White men living unlawfully with negro women must be taught that virtuous society will not endure the evil which the law has especially condemned and provided punishment for."[33] A Negro girl who worked during the nineties in a hotel patronized by travelling salesmen and construction workers building Clemson College complained that her job "meant constant battle against unwanted advances, a studied ignoring of impudent glances, insulting questions."[34] The informal relationships of white men and Negro women, however, received practically no

27 *Ibid.*
28 *Acts and Joint Resolutions* (1879), p. 3.
29 Hogan, *International Review*, VIII (February, 1880), 119.

30 Columbia *Daily Register*, June 10, 1881.
31 Charleston *News and Courier*, October 31, 1881.
32 Charleston *New Era*, July 1, 1882.
33 Columbia *Daily Register*, September 5, 1879.
34 Hunter, *A Nickle and a Prayer*, p. 32.

mention in the press, and there seems to have been little will to bring the power of the law to bear against those who participated in such liaisons.

When it was sought in 1895 to write the law against interracial marriage into the new state constitution, Robert Smalls sought to back the white delegates into a corner by introducing an amendment providing that any white person guilty of cohabiting with a Negro should be barred from holding office, and further that the child of such a relationship should bear the name of its father and inherit property the same as if legitimate.[35] James Wigg, sharp-tongued delegate from Beaufort, noting the consternation that Smalls had thrown into the white delegates, commented that the "coons" had the dogs up the tree for a change and intended to keep them there until they admitted that they must accept such a provision.[36] The Columbia *State* felt that the white delegates had no choice but to swallow the dose concocted by Smalls with the best grace they could muster.[37] Ben Tillman, not entirely unsympathetic with Smalls' proposal, introduced a substitute amendment to punish miscegenation as a crime in order to "protect negro women against the debauchery of white men degrading themselves to the level of black women," but the convention refused to accept either his substitute or Smalls' original motion.[38] It contented itself with a simple provision against intermarriage, leaving the punishment to the discretion of the legislature.[39]

The issue of miscegenation also posed for the convention the delicate question of defining "Negro." The legislative committee's report spoke of "one eighth or more" Negro ancestry. One delegate proposed that this be changed to read "any" Negro ancestry. George Tillman, with rare realism, opposed reducing the quota below one-eighth, pointing out that he was acquainted with several families in his Congressional District which had a small degree of Negro ancestry, yet had furnished able soldiers to the Confederacy and were now accepted in white society. He did not want to see such families needlessly embarrassed. In addition he made the astounding claim that there was not one pure-blooded Caucasian on the floor of the convention. He maintained that all had ancestors from at least one of the colored races, though not necessarily the Negro race. Therefore he called for a provision that would define "Negro" as a person with one-fourth or more Negro ancestry.[40] But as finally included in the constitution the provision was allowed to stand as reported by the committee, with the limitation set at one-eighth.[41]

The issue of segregation in public carriers was not early raised by Democratic politicians. Robert Smalls in 1884 found cause for pride in the fact that the state of South Carolina had a statute providing that Negroes should get equal accommodations for equal fares on the railroads of the state.[42] T. McCants Stewart in the following year reported that "a colored lady or gentleman with a first-class ticket rides with Senator Hampton, and neither is hurt; nor, so far as I know, is amalgamation encouraged in my native State because Negroes dine with whites in a railroad saloon and ride with them in the same car."[43] As late as 1895 Ben Tillman rode from a station near Augusta to

---

[35] Columbia *State*, October 3, 1895.
[36] *Ibid.*, October 4, 1895.
[37] *Ibid.*
[38] *Ibid.*
[39] *Constitution of 1895*, Art. III, Sec. 33.

[40] Columbia *Daily Register*, October 17, 1895.
[41] *Constitution of 1895*, Art. III, Sec. 33.
[42] *Congressional Record*, XVI (48th Congress, 2d Session), 316.
[43] New York *Age*, April 18, 1885.

Columbia, side by side with a Negro reporter, while he explained to him his plans for the disfranchisement of Negroes.[44] Arguing against Jim Crow, the Charleston *News and Courier* found the *reductio ad absurdum* in the argument that if segregation were required on the railway cars it would have to be provided also in separate waiting rooms and separate eating facilities in the stations, a prohibitive item of expense.[45] Nevertheless, the absence of any formal provision for segregation did not prevent its occasional application. A Negro passenger complained in 1887 that he was unable to get a cup of coffee in the station at Florence because he was unable to produce his own cup from which to drink it.[46]

The repeal of the state civil rights law in 1889, removing the statutory prohibition against segregation was the signal for the introduction of legislation to give segregation the sanction of law. In the legislative session of 1889 the first bill was introduced providing for segregation on railways of the state.[47] Thereafter it became a perennial issue until passed in 1898. The inertia of white public opinion was one reason for the hesitation of the legislature to pass such a measure, but the strong opposition of the railway companies, made effective through conservative Low Country senators, was the greatest factor in preventing its passage.[48] The *News and Courier,* sympathetic to the railroad viewpoint, held in 1897 that the measure would increase "the burdens and troubles of the already over-burdened railroads without due cause," and expressed the opinion "that we have no more need for a Jim Crow car system this year than we had last year, and a great

deal less need than we had twenty and thirty years ago."[49]

Jim Crow bills naturally found opposition among Negroes. The first measures provided for segregation only in first-class cars, and James Wigg pointed out that a poor man would have to seat his wife in a second-class car along with the Negroes. "If it is degrading to the rich," he asked, "why is it not degrading to the poor?"[50] In states that had already adopted similar Jim Crow provisions it had become customary for white men who wished to smoke, drink, or otherwise disport themselves to retire to the second-class cars. The members of the Claflin faculty, in an address to the legislature asked:

Why should you, who treasure the honor of your weaker sex more highly than life wish to subject our helpless children, our wives, our mothers, our daughters to the insults and vile actions of drunken and vulgar men and more vulgar women. . . .

Think, gentlemen, that while we have no rights, we have at least feelings. Spare us this injustice. Follow the golden rule. Legislate, we pray you, for the whole people. Give greater police power, if you please, to the train officers; but save our mothers, our wives, our daughters from further humiliation and insults.[51]

In 1898 a bill finally got through the senate by one vote despite an unfavorable report by the senate's railroad committee. The measure became effective on September 1, 1898. It provided that separate first-class coaches or apartments, "separated by a substantial partition," should be provided for passengers on all railroads more than forty miles in length.

[44] Charleston *News and Courier,* April 26, 1895.
[45] *Ibid.,* January 25, 1898.
[46] *Ibid.,* June 28, 1887.
[47] Columbia *Daily Register,* December 19, 1889.
[48] *Ibid.,* December 15, 1894.

[49] *Ibid.,* February 25, 1897.
[50] Columbia *Daily Register,* December 9, 1891.
[51] Address to the General Assembly, signed by seven members of the faculty of Claflin University, in Columbia *State,* January 17, 1898.

It also provided that equal accommodations should be supplied to both races.[52] Shortly after its effective date one conductor noticed that Negroes generally preferred second-class accommodation to those in the Jim Crow apartments or cars. He suggested that the eventual solution would be elimination of the second-class cars and the provision of separate cars for white and colored.[53] In 1900 the law was amended to require separate coaches for the two races except on trains that did not require more than one coach. The law did not apply to extraordinary emergencies, nurses attending the children or sick of the other race, prisoners and guards, or to freight and through-vestibuled trains.[54]

Segregation rapidly became an established and unquestioned fact in all the institutions and relationships of the two races. Judge Christie Benet, presiding over a session of court at Beaufort in 1899, called attention to the fact that whites and Negroes were sitting together on the courtroom benches and directed that one side of the room be allotted to whites and the other side to Negroes. "God Almighty never intended," he said, "that the two races should be mixed. . . ."[55] Thus, by the end of the century a new social arrangement had been established by statute, by custom, by direction of the dominant whites, and by the institutional segregation of schools, churches, and private organizations. Slavery was replaced as an instrument of maintaining the subordination of the Negro by a caste system based on race under which white and black seldom came into personal contact except in the relationship of employer and laborer.

[52] *Acts and Joint Resolutions* (1898), pp. 777–78.

[53] Charleston *News and Courier*, October 11, 1898.

[54] *Acts and Joint Resolutions* (1900), p. 427.

[55] Yorkville *Enquirer*, January 11, 1899.

Vernon Lane Wharton: JIM CROW LAWS AND MISCEGENATION

Key factual material on the origins of segregation is contained in Wharton's The Negro in Mississippi, 1865–1890. *Two selections from that book follow. Footnotes are included to allow the reader to date textual references. For many years before his death in 1964 Professor Wharton was Dean of the College of Arts and Sciences at Southwestern Louisiana University.*

JIM CROW LAWS

THE DETERMINATION of the mass of the whites to set up legal differences between the races was further demonstrated in the enactment in 1865 of the first "Jim Crow" law in the South. The few Negroes who traveled on public conveyances before the war had generally been directly in the service of their masters. There was little or no objection to their presence.[1] With the coming of free-

[1] Jackson *Clarion*, February 18, 1866.

From Vernon Lane Wharton, *The Negro in Mississippi, 1865–1890, James Sprunt Studies in History and Political Science*, Vol. XXVIII (1947), pp. 230–33, 227–29. Reprinted by permission of the University of North Carolina Press.

dom, all this was changed. Large numbers of the freedmen now took advantage of the opportunity to move about from place to place, and there can be no doubt that in the crowded cars the low standards of sanitation observed by most of them added greatly to objections based on racial difference. The better railroads immediately adopted the custom of refusing to Negroes admission to the first-class, or "ladies'" cars.[2] On smaller roads, which did not carry the two classes of cars, the freedmen, although they paid full fare, were relegated to old cars, freight cars, or open platforms.[3] The law approved by the Governor of the state in November, 1865, simply gave legality to a practice which the railroads had already adopted. According to its provisions it became unlawful for an employee of any railroad in the state to allow "any freedman, negro, or mulatto, to ride in any first class passenger cars, set apart, or used by, and for white persons. . . ." The law was not to apply to Negroes traveling with their mistresses in the capacity of nurses.[4] It is to be noticed that under this law those whites who were unable to pay first-class fares, or who did not choose to do so, continued to travel with the Negroes. White men also continued to use the second-class car for smoking, drinking, and impolite conversation. These circumstances not only led to racial difficulties, but also brought discomfort to the small number of cultured Negroes, of both sexes, who were forced to travel in such surroundings.[5] Although the law applied only to railroads, the principle which it recognized was followed on passenger boats, in theaters, and in a number of other places of public entertainment.[6]

With the assembly of the legislature of 1870, a number of the Negro members, especially Senators Robert Gleed and William Gray, set to work to prevent by law any discrimination against those of their race on public conveyances. After several disappointments, they succeeded in gaining enough votes from the reluctant white Republicans to secure the passage of such a law in June,[7] and to retain it in the revised code in the following April.[8] The law provided that the right of any citizen to travel on any railroad, steamboat, other water craft, or stage coach was not to be denied or infringed. Any employee who refused that right, or who should "compel, or attempt to compel, any person or persons to occupy any particular seat, or any particular part" of such conveyances on account of race or color was made subject to a fine, a suit for damages by the person injured, and a term in the county jail.[9] In spite of its stringent provisions, the law had almost no effect. The captains of the river boats, the chief means of travel in the black counties, simply disregarded the law. On the trains, practically all of the Negroes, either from choice or economic necessity, continued to ride in the second-class cars.[10] A conductor in 1871 did not hesitate to ask James Lynch, secretary of state, to leave the "ladies'" car. Lynch immediately complied with the request.[11]

The failure of the general railroad act

[2] W. Reid, *After the War*, p. 421.
[3] *Ibid.*, note, p. 386.
[4] Mississippi *Session Laws*, 1865, p. 231.
[5] Mississippi *Weekly Pilot*, May 15, 1870, August 31, 1872.
[6] J. T. Trowbridge, *The South*, p. 352; Natchez *Tri-Weekly Democrat*, July 9, 1867.
[7] Mississippi *Weekly Pilot*, May 15, 28, June 4, 1870; Jackson *Semi-Weekly Clarion*, June 10, 1870.
[8] Jackson *Clarion*, April 14, 1871.
[9] Mississippi *Revised Code*, 1871, sections 2731–2732.
[10] J. S. McNeily, "War and Reconstruction in Mississippi," *P.M.H.S.C.S.*, II, 414–415.
[11] Hinds County *Gazette*, January 25, 1871.

did not prevent efforts of the Negroes to extend its provisions in a civil rights bill in the next session of the legislature. After a great deal of argument, some chicanery, and much discomfort on the part of the white Republicans, this bill finally failed by one vote to gain the approval of the senate.[12] Renewed agitation in the following year finally gained its passage. In essence, it extended the provisions of the railroad act to cover hotels, inns, and theaters and other places of public amusement, and added to the penalties a requirement for the forfeiture of the charter of any corporation that violated the act.[13]

Early in the following year, a decision in a test case in Vicksburg exempted from the provisions of the act all organizations save those which held a public charter.[14] Although a Supreme Court decision a little later in the year upheld the act in its limited sense,[15] it enjoyed little more success than its predecessors. Here and there a few Negroes braved public wrath by refusing to leave sections set apart for the other race,[16] but such cases were rare. Congressman John R. Lynch, requested to leave a white table in a railroad dining room at Holly Springs, retired without protest.[17]

By 1888, this working arrangement was not satisfactory to the white-line element of the hill counties which was rapidly increasing its influence in the state. The first- and second-class arrangement, with a practical white monopoly of the first-class accommodations, did not sufficiently emphasize racial differences. The result was the passage of "an act to promote the comfort of passengers on railroad trains." This ordered all railroads carrying passengers in the state to provide "equal but separate accommodations" for the races.[18] A few days later, a supplementary act made this regulation applicable to sleeping car companies "so far as practicable," and authorized the railroad commissioners to designate and provide, if deemed proper, separate waiting rooms for the sexes and the races.[19]

Since it was the determination of a large mass of the white population to apply a code of racial distinctions to all possible situations and places in which the races might be thrown together, it is apparent that the matter was not entirely a problem of law. The development of a ritual to be followed by whites and blacks under varying conditions was a slow and tedious process. In the early part of the period, most of the saloons served whites and Negroes at the same bar. Many of the restaurants, using separate tables, served both races in the same room. By 1890, such cases were practically unknown. On May 21, 1879, the Negroes of Jackson, after a parade of their fire company, gave a picnic in Hamilton Park. On the night of May 29, "the ladies of the Episcopal Church" used Hamilton Park for a *fete*.[20] After their picnic, the Negroes went to Angelo's Hall for a dance. This same hall was used for white dances and parties, and was frequently the gathering place of Democratic conventions. By 1890, both the park and the hall were closed to the Negroes. Throughout the state common cemeteries, usually in separate portions,

[12] J. S. McNeily, "War and Reconstruction in Mississippi," *P.M.H.S.C.S.*, II, 431.

[13] Mississippi *Session Laws*, 1873, pp. 66–69.

[14] Hinds County *Gazette*, March 19, May 7, 1873; Vicksburg *Herald*, May 8, 1873.

[15] Vicksburg *Times and Republican*, May 7, 1873; Gilbert Stephenson, *Race Distinctions in American Law*, p. 134.

[16] Hinds County *Gazette*, February 11, 1874.

[17] *Ibid.*, July 15, 1874.

[18] Mississippi *Session Laws*, 1888, p. 48.

[19] *Ibid.*, 1888, pp. 45–48.

[20] Jackson *Weekly Clarion*, May 21, June 4, 1879.

held the graves of both whites and Negroes. In 1890, the city of Jackson, in line with a policy which was being adopted all over the state, established a new cemetery, and ruled that on and after January 1, 1891, all interments of Negroes should take place in it.[21]

Sidewalks, depot platforms, and promenades offered a more difficult problem. The code held that the Negro on a sidewalk must always give way to the white man, especially if the white was accompanied by a woman. "Jostling" sometimes led to beatings, shootings, or lynchings.[22] Negroes were warned to keep their distance and mind their language in public gathering places, or the citizens would "make a striking example of somebody."[23] Negroes at Natchez received instructions that of the promenades along the river, the bluff to the right of Main Street was "for the use of whites, for ladies and children and nurses—the central Bluff between Main street and State for bachelors and the colored population, and the lower promenade for the whites." There was no law on the subject, but the people would see to it that the warning was heeded.[24] The question as to what streets were to be used by white and Negro children in their play also demanded attention.[25]

The Negro must also learn to be careful in his expression of an opinion, and to avoid unfavorable criticism of white people or white enterprises. In 1886, the Tougaloo *Quarterly* carried an article entitled "Life Incidents of One of Our Boys." Some of these incidents were not flattering to the white people from whose state treasury came money for the school. The president escaped censure by promising careful examination of all future material.[26] A "little popinjay didapper of a half coon who [had] learned to spell 'baker' at the expense of the tax-payers" wrote to a Negro paper in New Orleans letters which contained "several mischievous lies on the good people of Woodville and Wilkinson County." The editor of the *Clarion-Ledger* demanded that he be identified, strapped across a log, soundly whipped, and made to leave the county.[27]

Newspapers had their own peculiar problems. The Natchez *Courier* took Negro advertising,[28] the *Clarion* refused to handle it without a distinguishing label.[29] Some newspapers of the state carried formal notices of Negro weddings, but the editor of the Hinds County *Gazette* would have none of them.[30] The name used for the race varied with circumstances, usually it was "the negroes," or "our laboring population." When a fusion ticket against Greenbackers or Populists was to be promoted, the terms were "the colored population," or "our colored citizens"; in times of bad feelings the expressions "niggers," "coons," "kullud pussons," and "blacks" were used. In normal times throughout a large part of the period, Negroes of prominence were given the title "Hon." or "Mr." by most of the papers of the state. By 1890, however, this usage had almost entirely disappeared.

Thus, within twenty-five years after the end of the war, a new code had come to

21 Jackson *Clarion-Ledger*, January 1, 1891.
22 Vicksburg *Herald*, April 9, 1873; Hinds County *Gazette*, August 18, 1888; *Senate Miscellaneous Documents*, no. 166, 50th Congress, 1st session, pp. 88, 99, 170.
23 Hinds County *Gazette*, August 18, 1888.
24 Natchez *Daily Courier*, May 29, 1866.
25 Hinds County *Gazette*, March 8, 1871; Mississippi *Weekly Pilot*, March 23, 1871.

26 Jackson *Weekly Clarion*, June 16, 1886.
27 Jackson *Clarion-Ledger*, October 17, 1889.
28 Natchez *Daily Courier*, May 31, 1866.
29 Meridian *Clarion*, November 18, 1865.
30 Hinds County *Gazette*, March 9, 1866.

replace the slave code of 1857. Few of its provisions could be found in the statute books. Its application was at times capricious and unpredictable. But, in general, members of both races understood and observed its content. In almost any conceivable contact with a white man, there were certain forms of behavior which the black man must observe. The Negro, at last, was "in his place."

❊   ❊   ❊

MISCEGENATION

Under the ante-bellum plantation system, there was naturally a certain amount of sexual relationship between some of the owners, their sons, and overseers and the female slaves. The situation was seldom openly discussed. With proper discretion, such indulgence apparently did not seriously affect the relations of the white participant with others of his own social group. Among the Negroes, the mistress of the master often occupied a highly respected and coveted position.

In general, the small farmers and poor whites were strongly opposed to the easy-going tolerance displayed by the planting and professional groups toward such relationships. This attitude was another expression of their lack of economic and social security, and of their determination to emphasize the difference between the Negroes and themselves. It was to this feeling that such leaders as A. G. Brown appealed most effectively in their successful efforts to enlist the support of the non-slaveholders in the campaign for secession. Freedom for slaves, they said, would inevitably mean social equality; Negroes would obtain white girls in marriage, and soon all racial distinction would be lost.[31]

These small-farmer and poor-white

groups, who held a controlling influence over the legislature of 1865, took heed of their misgivings, and lost no time in writing into law their feelings on the question. A section of the Black Code, adopted in December, 1865, provided:

. . . it shall not be lawful for any freedman, free negro or mulatto to intermarry with any white person, nor for any white person to intermarry with any freedman, free negro or mulatto, and any person who shall so intermarry shall be deemed guilty of felony, and on conviction thereof shall be confined in the State penitentiary for life; and those shall be deemed freedmen, free negroes and mulattoes who are of pure negro blood, and those descended from a negro to the third generation inclusive, though one ancestor in each generation may have been a white person.[32]

Although it appears that a Northern white officer married a Negro woman in Vicksburg in January or February of 1866,[33] the first case under the law did not come up until June of that year. Ben ❊❊❊, a Negro who had been a soldier in the Federal army, married Mollie ❊❊❊, a white girl from Simpson County. A raid by county officers in the early hours of the morning of June 13 was followed by a trial of the couple before the circuit court. Found guilty, each was sentenced to serve six months in the county jail, and to pay a fine of five hundred dollars.[34]

Two months later, a Negro man and a young white woman from Leake County endeavored to be married in Vicksburg. The girl, who was the daughter of the former owner of the Negro, declared that she desired to marry him because she

---

[31] P. L. Rainwater, *Mississippi, Storm Center of Secession*, pp. 144–149.

[32] Mississippi *Session Laws,* regular session, 1865, p. 82.
[33] Natchez *Tri-Weekly Democrat*, February 24, 1866.
[34] Jackson *Clarion and Standard*, June 14, 1866; Hinds County *Gazette*, June 22, 1866. It is impossible to explain this sentence in terms of the penalty provided by the law.

loved him. Investigation revealed the fact that they had been having relations in defiance of the law, and the judge ordered that they be held for trial in the ensuing term of the criminal court.[35] It appears that the matter must have been hushed up in some fashion, as there is no further public record of the case. With the exception of the arrest in Vicksburg of a woman from Lauderdale County on the charge of cohabitation with a Negro,[36] there seems to have been no further application of the law.

The repeal by the legislature of 1870 of all laws involving racial discrimination was followed almost immediately by a case that attracted wide attention. A. T. Morgan, a cultured and formerly affluent planter from Ohio, who had been a member of the constitutional convention, was at the time a state senator, and later served as sheriff of Yazoo County, married a young octoroon teacher who had come down from New York. The state followed with interest the difficulties of their honeymoon journey, which included ejection from a bus in Louisville, Kentucky, and the printing of vulgar comments by Northern papers.[37] This marriage, the only one during the period which received wide attention, appears to have been happily maintained for many years after the couple left the state in 1876.

Another case which attracted some attention within the state was the marriage of Haskins Smith, mulatto member of the state legislature, to the daughter of the owner of the hotel in which Smith worked in Port Gibson. Although leading citizens of the community held Smith to be a good man and refused to be aroused over the matter, lower classes among the whites created a great deal of disturbance.[38] References to this marriage in a speech by a Negro in Vicksburg helped to bring about the overthrow of the Republican government in that city a little later in the summer.[39]

It is impossible to estimate how many interracial marriages occurred between more obscure people. It seems probable that there were not very many. Evidence that some did occur is offered by such small items as a passage in the diary of a pious Irish contractor in Claiborne County:

Confirmation at Chadenel I was discusted to see *Joe O Brian* as god father for Boys, he who has a lot of *Niger* Bastards & is now married to a ½ *Niger* wife What a scandle to me[40]

The restoration of Democratic control in the state in 1876 was followed by a return of legal prohibition of intermarriage of the races. Such marriages were declared to be "incestuous [sic] and void," and the parties participating were made subject to the penalties for incest. These included a maximum term of ten years in prison. For the purposes of the act, a Negro was any person who had one-fourth or more of Negro blood.[41]

Very few opportunities were found for the application of the law. In 1883, a

[35] Natchez *Tri-Weekly Democrat*, August 21, 1866, quoting the Vicksburg *Herald*, August 14, 1866.

[36] Jackson *Clarion*, August 26, 1866.

[37] J. S. McNeily, "War and Reconstruction in Mississippi," *P.M.H.S.C.S.*, II, 403; Hinds County *Gazette*, August 17, 1870; Mississippi *Weekly Pilot*, November 26, 1870; A. T. Morgan, *Yazoo*, pp. 345–351.

[38] *Senate Reports*, no. 527, 44th Congress, 1st session, pp. 159, 191–192.

[39] *Ibid.*, pp. 1312–1313, 1367; J. S. McNeily, "Climax and Collapse of Reconstruction in Mississippi," *P.M.H.S.*, XII, 297.

[40] Patrick Murphy, "Diary," vol. 16, Sunday, April 12, 1885, Patrick Murphy Papers.

[41] Mississippi *Code*, 1880, sections 1145–1147, The constitution of 1890, like the law of 1865, classified as a Negro any person having one-eighth or more of Negro blood.

white man in Rankin County, who had formerly been fined for unlawful cohabitation with a Negro woman, persuaded a Negro preacher to marry them.[42] Although the newspaper report predicted that he would receive a sentence to prison, no further mention of his case is to be found. In 1885, a resident of Hinds County, charged with incest on the grounds of his marriage to a Negro woman, received the maximum sentence of ten years.[43]

The abolition of the possibilities of legal marriage, which in any case would have involved very few individuals, did not do away with concubinage and unlawful cohabitation. The matter received little public attention, but now and then legal complications or violent tragedies revealed its existence.[44] It appears, however, that such relationships became steadily less frequent as time went on. The racial code of the poor white came more and more to be that of the public at large.

[42] Jackson *Weekly Clarion*, January 24, 1883.
[43] Raymond *Gazette*, August 1, 1885.

[44] Hinds County *Gazette*, May 27, June 3, 24, September 2, 1874, August 25, 1880; Jackson *Weekly Clarion*, August 9, 1882; A. T. Morgan, *op. cit.*, pp. 494–495.

Charles E. Wynes: SOCIAL ACCEPTANCE AND UNACCEPTANCE

> *Charles E. Wynes in 1961 published one of the first monographs to challenge the extent of fluidity in race relations which many readers saw in* The Strange Career of Jim Crow. *The following selection is from his book* Race Relations in Virginia, 1870–1902. *Dr. Wynes is now a Professor of History in the University of Georgia, Athens.*

A T THE same time that the Virginia Negro fought hopelessly for political equality, he struggled even more hopelessly for social equality. The Thirteenth Amendment to the Constitution had made his freedom a reality, but in the face of almost universal Southern opposition, the Fourteenth and Fifteenth Amendments never assured to him either equal protection under state laws or exercise of his vote without impediment. And, by the end of the century, Southern states no longer hesitated to pass laws which abridged privileges of the Negro and denied him the right to vote. The road from merely ignoring the Fourteenth and Fifteenth Amendments to openly flouting them, wound through thirty tortured years of Virginia history. Along the way, both Negroes and whites were puzzled by the inconsistencies which marked it, but the average white Virginian was far more determined that the Negro should not enjoy what was commonly termed social equality than he was determined that the Negro should not enjoy political equality. Even so, the most distinguishing factor in the complexity of social relations between the races, was that of inconsistency. From 1870–1900, there was no generally accepted code of racial mores. It is perhaps true that in a majority of the cases where a Negro presumed to demand equal treat-

From Charles E. Wynes, *Race Relations in Virginia, 1870–1902* (1961), pp. 68–83. Reprinted by permission of The University Press of Virginia.

ment — in hotels, restaurants, theatres, and bars, and even on the railroads — he was more likely to meet rejection than acceptance. But uncertainty led many Negroes to keep trying for acceptance, just as it led at least some whites to accept them. Acceptance by the whites of racial intermingling on the railroads was encouraged by the propensity of the Federal courts to award damages to Negroes who charged unequal treatment.

Perhaps the best summary of the treatment of Negroes on the railroads of not only Virginia, but of the entire South, is that of this contemporary, who wrote: "On most of the railroads in the South the negroes were expected and told to take a particular car in each train, and they usually did so; but the rule did not appear to be strictly enforced." Well-dressed Negroes, claimed this observer, sometimes traveled in the first-class cars, and the more poorly-dressed whites were sometimes found in the Negro car.[1]

Until the Federal Civil Rights Act of 1866 was passed, Virginia law did not permit Negroes to ride on public street cars. Following passage of that act, a suit was brought by a group of Negroes against a Richmond street railway company to test the validity of the practiced discrimination. The result was that the right of the Negroes to ride on street cars was recognized, but two classes of cars were established — one for white women and their escorts only, and one for all persons regardless of race or sex. After Military Reconstruction began, in 1867, Negroes were allowed to ride the street cars without even this discrimination. On the railroads, however, throughout the period 1865–1870, Negroes generally were made to ride in the smoking car.

This practice included Negro women and children as well as Negro men.[2]

As early as April, 1870, however, at least one Virginia railroad reportedly resorted to the use of a special or Jim Crow car for Negro passengers only, instead of assigning them indiscriminately to the smoking car. This was done by the Orange and Alexandria (now part of the Southern) Railroad. At the same time, the smoking car accommodating both races was retained.[3] To some Negroes, including Negro legislators, this was apparently an acceptable procedure. Negro opposition to discrimination by the railroads centered on the frequent practice of requiring them to ride in the smoking car, not on the use of Jim Crow cars, although there was, of course, opposition to that policy too. On January 5, 1871, a Negro member of the House of Delegates offered a resolution that a committee of three be appointed to consult with the owners of the various railroads operating in Virginia in regard to provision of special cars for the sole and exclusive use of Negro passengers. The response of the House was to reject the motion without even sending it to committee.[4] This action, however, represented not opposition to the principle of segregation, but rather it represented the belief that Negroes should continue to ride in the smoking cars.

Because many Negroes objected to leaving first-class cars to ride in the Jim Crow car or the smoking car, a number of suits charging violation of the Civil Rights Act and the Fourteenth Amendment were brought in the Federal courts during the early 1870's. In January, 1871,

[1] Harrison, "Studies in the South," *Atlantic Monthly*, L (1882), 626.

[2] Taylor, "Negro in the Reconstruction of Virginia," *Journal of Negro History*, XI (1926), 294.
[3] Richmond *Daily Dispatch*, April 8, 1870.
[4] *Journal of the House of Delegates, 1870–71*, p. 79.

a colored woman named Kate Cummings was awarded $1,100 damages by the U. S. Circuit Court in Richmond because she had been forcibly removed from a first-class car and made to ride in the smoking car. She had purchased a first-class ticket in New York for Lynchburg, Virginia, and had traveled first-class until she was between Washington, D. C. and Alexandria on the Orange and Alexandria line.[5] This line had begun the use of a "for colored only" car in 1870.[6] In January of 1871 the car for colored persons was either not attached to this train or was no longer being used, because one of the newspapers which reported the incident went on to advocate editorially the use of separate cars for Negroes instead of forcing them to ride in the smoking car.[7]

A number of similar cases arose the same year. J. J. Wright, Negro judge of the Supreme Court of South Carolina, purchased a first-class ticket in Charleston and rode in first-class cars in both that state and in North Carolina. But when he reached Clover Depot in Halifax county, Virginia, on the Richmond and Danville road, he was made to leave the first-class car on the personal order of Colonel Algernon S. Buford, president of the line. Wright sued the railroad for $5,000 damages but settled out of court for $1,250.[8] Also in 1871, James Sims, colored, was awarded $1,800 in damages against the Richmond, Fredericksburg, and Potomac Railroad and the Potomac Steamboat Company for being forced, in 1869, to leave the main saloon of the steamer *Keyport* even though he held a first-class ticket. Sims was a member of the Georgia legislature at the time and

was traveling from Washington, D. C. to Savannah, Georgia[9] Five years later, in 1876, a watchman at the Chesapeake and Ohio depot in Staunton was sentenced to four months imprisonment for putting a Negro woman out of the passengers' waiting room.[10] In May, 1871, a Negro had been evicted from a Richmond street car set apart for the use of white persons, but no legal action had been brought.[11]

After about the middle 1870's, the frequency of such incidents greatly decreased and did not increase again. Why this is so cannot readily be determined, but there are some probable reasons, which singly or together, tend to explain the anomaly. Following the end of Military Reconstruction, white Virginians were eager to reassert their old authority over their former slaves and resented the rights which the military commanders had allowed the Negro to exercise. The Negro, on the other hand, was determined to hold on to whatever rights he had been granted[12] and to expand them if possible in face of any white opposition. By the mid-1870's, the Conservatives had generally succeeded in putting the Negro in his place and had thoroughly consolidated their hold over both politics and the Negro. As a result, the Negro not only ceased to be a major political factor,[13] but also, in despair, ceased to insist upon being granted many of his rights.

In 1873–1874, Edward King traveled

[5] Richmond *Daily Dispatch*, January 28, 1871.
[6] *Ibid.*, April 8, 1870.
[7] Harrisonburg *Old Commonwealth*, February 1, 1871.
[8] *Ibid.*, April 19, 1871.

[9] Richmond *Daily Dispatch*, May 18–19, 1871.
[10] Taylor, "Negro in Reconstruction of Virginia," *Journal of Negro History*, XI (1926), 295.
[11] Richmond *Daily Dispatch*, May 31, 1871.
[12] These rights, however, did not include indiscriminate seating on the railroads. Taylor, "Negro in Virginia Reconstruction," *Journal of Negro History*, XI (1926), 294.
[13] Eckenrode, "History of Virginia Since 1865," p. 94; Morton, *Negro in Virginia Politics*, p. 96; Martin, "Negro Disfranchisement in Virginia," *Howard University Studies in the Social Sciences*, I, p. 89.

through the South gathering material for his book, *The Great South,* in which he spoke of "the car where the colored people were seated" on the Gordonsville to Lynchburg, Virginia train.[14] In 1882, a Virginia Negro newspaper referred to the "Jim Crow car" in the same breath with the "negro gallery."[15] That there were Jim Crow cars, some white Virginians ashamedly admitted, as did the *Loudoun Telephone,* in 1891: "Virginia cannot afford to have the Jim Crow car stand among her other products at the [Chicago] World's Fair."[16] W. E. B. DuBois, a student at Fisk University, Nashville, Tennessee, recalled in his autobiography (without specifically stating where) separation of the races on the railroads of the South, a practice which, he said, was just beginning.[17]

There is also evidence which indicates that racial incidents on the railroads decreased by the mid-1870's because large numbers of white Virginians, at least in some parts of the state, gradually became accustomed to Negroes riding in whatever cars and seats they chose. Thomas Wentworth Higginson, onetime abolitionist and commander of a Negro combat regiment in the Civil War, ob- served in 1878 that he "rode with colored people in first-class cars throughout Virginia and South Carolina, and in street cars in Richmond and Charleston."[18] In 1885, George W. Cable, critic of the South which he loved, wrote: "In Virginia they [*i.e.* the Negroes] may ride exactly as white people do and in the same cars."[19] That same year, T. McCants Stewart, a Negro newspaperman from Boston, Massachusetts, recorded how he rode in a railway car between Washington, D. C. and Petersburg, Virginia, which was so crowded that some white passengers had to sit on their luggage, while he retained his seat undisturbed by either white passengers or conductor.[20]

In the *Southern Workman,* published at The Hampton Institute, Hampton, Virginia, there appeared for many years a more or less regular column headed "Southern Sketches," and written by (Mrs.) Orra Langhorne. Born and reared in Harrisonburg, Virginia, she came of a family which, like that of her husband, had owned slaves before the Civil War. At the time her column appeared, she and her husband lived in Lynchburg, but she often returned to the Valley by way of Charlottesville and Staunton to visit relatives still living there. Traveling by rail on these trips, she gathered material for her column. She loved Virginia but was liberal-minded in that love, and one might say that she was emancipated from the Southern tradition. Warmly human

[14] King, *Great South,* p. 554. This was undoubt- edly the Orange and Alexandria Railroad, the line which in 1870 reportedly began using "for colored only" cars — Richmond *Daily Dispatch,* April 8, 1870.
[15] Richmond *Virginia Star,* November 11, 1882.
[16] Quoted in Sheldon, *Populism in the Old Do- minion,* p. 35.
[17] W. E. B. DuBois, *Dusk of Dawn: An Essay Toward an Autobiography of a Race Concept* (New York, 1940), p. 30. A Tennessee statute of 1881 provided for separate first-class accommo- dations for Negroes but left second-class cars unsegregated. Separation of the races on the railroads *by statute* was begun in the South in Florida, in 1887; Mississippi, 1888; Texas, 1889; Louisiana, 1890; and in Alabama, Arkansas, Kentucky, and Georgia in 1891 — Woodward, *Origins of the New South,* pp. 211 n.–212. Not till 1900 did Virginia provide by law for separa- tion of the races on the railroads.

[18] Thomas Wentworth Higginson, "Some War Scenes Revisited," *Atlantic Monthly,* XLII (July, 1878), 7.
[19] George W. Cable, "The Silent South," *Century Magazine,* XXX (1885), 685. This article and other similar material is also available in book form — Cable, *The Silent South* (New York, 1885); Cable, *The Negro Question,* edited by Arlin Turner (New York, 1958).
[20] Cited in C. Vann Woodward, *The Strange Career of Jim Crow* (New York, 1957, revised edition), p. 20.

and humanitarian in her interests, she was a shrewd observer who often saw behind a gilded façade. Writing in 1890 she noted, "Colored people move about a great deal these days, and so far as those seen in my frequent trips through Virginia, they travel in cars occupied by the general public without regard to 'race, color or previous condition of servitude.' "[21] The next year she wrote: "In the various journeyings of the last year, I have always seen colored people traveling in the ladies' car, and the street cars of various cities, and have never seen any objection made by white people to their doing so."[22]

Accurately summing up the racial discrimination policies of Virginia railroads, the Richmond *State* said, in 1890: ". . . it can be said of railway travel in Virginia, on some roads at least, that he [*i.e.* the Negro] occupies whatever seats he may be pleased to take in first-class car[s]."[23]

But of all the evidence which indicates that the two races did once ride side by side on some of the state's railways, the most convincing is that offered by the state railroad commissioner himself. In his annual report for 1891, J. C. Hill, state railroad commissioner, recommended that legislation be enacted to require separation of the races in railway cars. He proposed that Virginia adopt a law similar to that of Alabama, which required provision of separate cars or compartments for each race. Noting that the question had been discussed for several years, he pointed out that the use of second-class tickets by some of the Virginia railroads had been found to be inadequate to accomplish separation of the races. Neither, he admitted, did all

the railways companies in the state employ the second-class rate for separating the races.[24] Undoubtedly the matter had been discussed in some quarters for several years, as Commissioner Hill claimed, but it was a fact that none of the earlier annual reports of the railroad commissioner (dating from 1877) contained any such proposal for separation of the races.[25] Hill had been commissioner since 1887. He was still in that office when the Virginia statute of 1900 providing for separation of the races on the railroads was adopted, but only in 1891 did he ever recommend such legislation. Although it would be difficult to prove a connection, this fact should be viewed alongside the fact that the previous year (1890) had seen the inauguration of Gov. Philip W. McKinney, a man who showed little sympathy for the Negro, and who as a result was the most unpopular among Negroes of all the Virginia governors of this period.[26] Immediately after McKinney took office, Hill presented his annual report containing no recommendations for discrimination on trains. But a year later — the year of Hill's recommendation — McKinney's views and policies were much clearer. Hill's was a political office, and as shown by his long tenure in office he obviously knew how to follow the currently popular political line. Further testimony to his adroitness was his remaining in office throughout the O'Ferrall administration (1894–1898), for no Virginia governor since the Civil War was more popular with the Negroes or

---

21 Orra Langhorne, "Southern Sketches," *Southern Workman*, August, 1890.

22 *Ibid.*, August, 1891.

23 Richmond *State*, January 7, 1890.

24 *Fifteenth Annual Report of the Railroad Commissioner of the State of Virginia* (Richmond, 1891), p. VIII.

25 *Annual Report[s] of the Railroad Commissioner*, 1877–1890.

26 See the Negro newspaper, Richmond *Planet*, 1890–1893, inclusive, and *Planet*, March 23, 1895; also see *Appletons' Annual Cyclopedia* (1890), p. 850.

did more to protect them from the violence of lynch law and assure them justice before the courts than did O'Ferrall.[27]

The majority of the evidence indicates that by the end of the nineteenth century it was customary for the races to ride together on most of the railroads of Virginia without confinement to either a Jim Crow car or the smoking car. True, there were exceptions to this practice, but as the century wore on to a close, those exceptions became fewer and fewer. By 1900, instead of referring to "the car where the Negroes rode," or "the smoking car where the Negroes were," white Virginians spoke of the "present system" when they objected to mixing of the races on trains.[28] How strongly the mass of white Virginians objected to mixing of the races on the railroads cannot readily be determined. But evidence supporting the contention that the railroad segregation statute of 1900 was passed in response to popular demand extending over a number of years is indeed slight and unreliable.[29] Even the conservative

newspapers fail to reflect the alleged popular demand till late in 1899 and early in 1900. A number of racial incidents occurred on the railroads in rapid succession, and they were blown up by those newspapers into "state-wide demand for a railroad segregation statute."

One newspaper claimed that a general demand for separate cars arose throughout the state following an incident which took place in December of 1899. A drunken Negro sat down by a white woman on a Richmond-Petersburg train, and a white man forced him to move. (At the time there were also other Negroes in the same car[30] — further substantiation that the races did at one time customarily ride together in Virginia.) Shortly after, a fight occurred between two Negroes and several white men on board a Chesapeake and Ohio train bound from the west of the state to Richmond. The cause was one of the Negroes' allegedly picking up a cane belonging to a white man near whom he was sitting.[31] Such incidents had undoubtedly occurred before, creating little if any more disturbance than would have been caused by a drunken white man sitting by a white woman or by a white man allegedly stealing another's cane. Weight was added to the case for segregation, however, in an alleged incident involving Virginia Governor J. Hoge Tyler. While on his way by train to Atlanta, Georgia, in late 1899, Tyler reportedly awoke in the morning in his sleeping compartment to find "a negro opposite him, above him, and in front of him."[32] Within three months after this incident, the Virginia legislature enacted

[27] See the Negro newspaper, Richmond *Planet*, 1894–1897, inclusive, but especially the issue of March 23, 1895; also see *Proceedings of the Negro Protective Association*, Jackson Papers; and Morton, *Negro in Virginia Politics*, pp. 139–140.

[28] Richmond, *Twice A Week Times*, January 12, 1900.

[29] This is the contention of Morton, *Negro in Virginia Politics*, p. 141. As evidence Morton cites the Governor's Message to the General Assembly, 1891–1892. The governor at that time was Philip W. McKinney, who was not noted for friendliness toward the Negro, and who was in consequence unpopular with the Negro —Richmond *Planet*, 1890–1893, inclusive and *Appletons' Annual Cyclopedia* (1890), p. 850. It was also during McKinney's administration in which there was made the only recommendation by the State Railroad Commissioner that the races be separated on the railroads — *Report of the Railroad Commissioner*, 1891, p. VIII. The year of this recommendation corresponds with that of the governor's message cited by Morton.

[30] Richmond *Twice A Week Times*, January 12, 1900.

[31] *Ibid.*, January 9, 1900.

[32] Quoted in Writers' Program of the WPA, *Negro in Virginia*, p. 241. Source of the quotation not stated.

the law of 1900 *requiring* railroads operating in the state to furnish separate cars or coaches for the white and Negro races. In 1906, after experimenting with a law *authorizing* and *empowering* companies operating street cars to separate the races, a law was enacted *requiring* separation of the races on the street cars.[33] The famous *Plessy vs. Fergusson* Supreme Court decision of 1896 gave further impetus to the case for segregation. In this celebrated case, the court upheld the legality of an 1890 Louisiana statute which required provision of "separate but equal" accommodations for the two races on the railroads of the state. Soon that principle was to lend the legal basis to the myriad Southern Jim Crow laws. It is significant that Virginia waited for four years after this decision before enacting her separate railroad accommodations statute, and that the decision itself seemed to prompt no popular demand for racial separation.

Thus in thirty years the Negro had moved from the railway smoking car and a few Jim Crow cars to acceptance in first-class accommodations on most Virginia railroads, and then back to the Jim Crow car in every case. His was an odyssey of sorrow, of hope, and finally despair, since much that he had gained since 1865, including the suffrage and the recognized right to ride the trains and street cars as an equal, was swept away from him by a rash of legislation based upon white supremacy.

Much less successful than the Negro's search for equality of treatment on the state's railroads was his search for equal preferment in restaurants, hotels, bars, and theatres. Only in isolated cases did he meet with acceptance. Insistence upon these rights in nearly all instances met with cold rejection or physical eviction. However, it must be recognized that, unlike the situation of the railroads, there were very few public hostels or places of amusement from which Negroes sought service. In those years, anyone who journeyed more than a few miles from home almost always traveled by train, including poor whites and Negroes. But the Negroes, poor, ignorant, and often unaware of such luxuries, generally did not seek admittance to public establishments providing personal services or amusements. It was easy to rebuff the few who did. Besides, the majority of those seeking these things were travelers or visitors from outside the state, who were not prone to make an issue of discrimination they met only in passing. An out-of-state Negro visitor's being refused service in a Virginia restaurant was quite a different matter from that same visitor's buying a first-class railroad ticket in New York, for instance, only to be refused first-class accommodations when the train reached Virginia.

Throughout this period, public inns and hotels did not admit Negroes unless they catered solely to a Negro clientele.[34] In July, 1874, James Hayne Rainey, Negro congressman from South Carolina, entered a hotel dining room in Suffolk and was promptly thrown out forcibly.[35] Rare indeed were such incidents as that related in 1885 by T. McCants Stewart, the Northern Negro newspaperman. Leaving a train on which he had ridden without any evidence of discrimination, Stewart entered a railroad station dining room south of Petersburg, "bold as a lion," and sat down at a table with white people. He was politely served while the

---

[33] *Acts of the General Assembly of the State of Virginia, 1899–1900*, pp. 236–237; *Code of Virginia* (1904), p. 681; *Code of Virginia* (1919), I, p. 1595.

[34] Taylor, "Negro in the Reconstruction of Virginia," *Journal of Negro History*, XI (1926), 296.
[35] Samuel Denny Smith, *The Negro in Congress, 1870–1901* (Chapel Hill, N. C., 1940), p. 47.

white diners appeared not to notice him.[36] It should be remembered that the station dining room which Stewart entered was on a railroad which apparently did not resort to racial discrimination on its trains. The dining room probably belonged to the railroad or else catered to the railroad's passengers. Hence this incident becomes much less indicative of any policy of non-discrimination followed by Virginia restaurants. It does, however, indicate that at least one of the railroads which gave Negroes equal treatment on their trains gave them the same treatment in station dining rooms.

In an attempt to protect the Negro from discrimination on public conveyances, in restaurants, hotels, theatres, and other places of amusement, Congress passed the Supplementary Civil Rights Act of 1875. Forbidding discrimination because of "race, color or previous condition of servitude," the new law was a mere irritant to the South, which proceeded to violate it with impunity. Nevertheless, most Southerners were relieved when, in 1883, the Supreme Court declared it unconstitutional. An Arkansas newspaper commented: "Society is a law unto itself which in matters social in nature overrides the statutes. Against its decrees the written law is powerless."[37] As far as the Civil Rights Act was concerned, that statement was correct, because the Supreme Court decision held, in effect, that Congress had no power to legislate in the area of social rights for the Negro.[38] This court decision was of little practical import, because as noted

above, the South had violated the Civil Rights Act with impunity and as *The Nation* pointed out at the time of the law's passage, few Negroes sought to use the hotels and other public places anyway.[39] The New York *Tribune* observed that the law had done nothing except "irritate public feeling and keep alive antagonism between the races," because few Negroes could afford to bring suit in court even if done an injustice. Besides, said the *Tribune*, Negroes were not disposed to force themselves into hotels and the better theatre seats.[40]

As the *Tribune* claimed, Negroes generally did not insist upon sitting in the better theatre seats. Instead, they usually went without question to the gallery or other portion set aside for them. J. B. Harrison noted how Negroes were ushered to a gallery at public and theatrical functions in Norfolk and Richmond. If they insisted, however, they were permitted to sit in the main auditorium unless it was so crowded that they could not sit by themselves in the back or to one side, as they voluntarily did. Then they were directed, but apparently not forced, to go to the gallery; Harrison was told that if they insisted upon sitting among the whites, all the whites near them would have moved.[41] A week-long disturbance was created in Richmond in 1886 when a Negro member of the New York delegation to the Knights of Labor annual convention entered a theatre with white friends and sat down in the midst of the whites. Several white people left the theatre rather than remain seated near him.[42] A similar incident in Richmond in 1875 concerned two very light-skinned mulattoes attending the play

---

[36] Cited in Woodward, *Strange Career of Jim Crow*, p. 20.

[37] Quoted in John Hope Franklin, "History of Racial Segregation in the United States," *Annals of the American Academy of Political and Social Science*, CCCIV (March, 1956), 5.

[38] L. E. Murphy, "The Civil Rights Law of 1875," *Journal of Negro History*, XII (April, 1927), 126.

[39] Cited in *Ibid.*, 124.

[40] Cited in *Ibid.*, 125.

[41] Harrison, "Studies in the South," *Atlantic Monthly*, L (1882), 626.

[42] Richmond *Daily Dispatch*, October 5, 7, 8, 9, 10, 13, 1886.

Davy Crockett. When on the point of being forced to retire to the colored section, one of them left the theatre. When some of the men congregated in a saloon across the street after the play, a fight ensued between a John Snellings and a young man described as being "well known" in Richmond business circles, because the latter admitted that he had bought the ticket for one of the Negroes. The *Dispatch* did not name the "well known" businessman.[43] In Bedford (then known as Bedford City) in 1891, Sandy Hadue, colored, presented reserved tickets for himself and a colored companion at the local opera house, but was directed to the section set aside for Negroes, because Negroes had "never before occupied those [*i.e.* the reserved] seats."[44] The only public entertainments at which the Negro was sure of meeting no racial discrimination were circuses or other carnival-like events usually found in the smaller towns.[45]

Discrimination extended even to the use of public buildings for all-Negro official functions. A request to use the Harrisonburg town hall for graduation exercises in 1884 for the local colored school was firmly refused. Many white people attended the same commencement when held at the Negro school,[46] however, and in this same Valley town, both white and black were kept in one almshouse.[47] Whether they dined and lived together is not clear.

Lewis H. Blair, Richmond business man and outspoken liberal, accurately summed up the situation in his forthright book:

In the capital of our great country, the respectable negro, though not welcomed, is admitted to the best hotels, to the best seats in theatres . . . and in presidential receptions he meets with no humiliating discriminations; yet when we come south as far as Richmond . . . we seem to be in a different country, we seem to be transplanted from a world of equality where worth makes the man to a land of caste where birth makes him. In Richmond a riot is threatened when it is thought that a negro member of a Brooklyn white lodge intends occupying in company with his white brother, a first-class seat in the theatre. The hotels, except under extraordinary pressure [*sic*] drive negroes from their doors; . . . and if a negro with his wife . . . were to attend the governor's public reception, they would in a few minutes be the only guests, or they would be frozen, if not driven out.[48]

It is significant, however, that Blair claimed Richmond hotels drove Negroes from their doors, "except under extraordinary pressure." This statement implies that they *were* accepted in some instances. No other evidence in support of this has been found, but this does not mean that some Negroes were not admitted to the hotels, for the newspapers and the other contemporary records of that day were prone to publicize Negro rejection, not acceptance. Still, as Blair intimated, such instances were rare.

It was an exceptional instance when white and black met socially on the Negro's own ground, such as the private Hampton Institute. Here, at the African Methodist annual conference of 1879, General Samuel C. Armstrong, principal

---

[43] *Ibid.*, March 9, 1875.
[44] Richmond *Weekly Times*, December 31, 1891.
[45] Taylor, "Negro in the Reconstruction of Virginia," *Journal of Negro History*, XI (1926), 296.
[46] Hampton, *Southern Workman*, September, 1884.
[47] *Ibid.*, October, 1886.

[48] Blair, *Prosperity of the South Dependent Upon the Elevation of the Negro*, pp. 60–61. Blair was important enough for the conservative Lyon G. Tyler (editor) to list in the *Encyclopedia of Virginia Biography* (New York, 1915), III, p. 185, but it is no wonder that he was spoken of as having views which would "never achieve popularity south of the Potomac."

of the (then) Hampton Normal School, told delegates that in May, 1878, former slave-holders had dined with colored men and women at the Hampton examinations of that year.[49]

Rarer still were instances where the white man met the black man privately and socially. In 1884, the Rockingham county superintendent of schools, a Readjuster appointee, entertained at dinner in his home a Negro minister, the brother of one of his teachers. For this, the press and the populace heaped abuse upon him.[50] Governor Charles T. O'Ferrall (1894–1898) as staunch a friend as the Negro had in official position between 1865 and 1900, nevertheless drew the line on social relations with him. While he might do all he could to assure justice and prevent lynch violence,[51] the governor was not prepared to meet the Negro socially. In 1895, O'Ferrall received a visiting state delegation from Massachusetts unaware that there was to be a Negro in the group. To Massachusetts State Senator Thomas W. Darling, who had headed the delegation, he later wrote:

The time has not come when I would knowingly invite a committee of any kind in which there was a colored man to dine or lunch at my private house or the Gubernatorial Mansion. . . . candor requires me to say that if it had been intimated to me that a colored man was in your party my attentions would have been much more formal than they were and you would have been received at my Executive Office and not at the Mansion; for

I draw the line on the Negro at the social circle or anywhere else that suggests even a semblance of social equality.[52]

It was plain to the Negroes that socially they were unwanted, and as a consequence most of them simply did not insist upon equal social privileges even when they were in a position to do so. The following particular incident is of little significance in itself, but it does indicate how *many* Negroes meekly accepted the position of an inferior status. In Wise county of far-Southwest Virginia, there lived a former slave named Dan Richmond. His home was on Black Mountain near present-day Big Stone Gap. Places to stop overnight in that area were far apart, and on at least one occasion a white man requested lodging for the night. Richmond received him hospitably and gave him a clean bed in a room by himself. He was served a "delicious and substantial" meal at a separate table before Richmond and his family ate. All offer of payment was refused.[53]

The observations of contemporaries from abroad all bore out this general picture, although their observations were usually drawn from the broader American scene. The distinguished English historian Edward A. Freeman observed: "I need hardly say that I never met a negro at any American gentleman's table."[54] The French *Comte* Alessandro Zannini was so struck by the practice of segregation in the United States in the early 1880's that he wrote (in *De L'Atlantique Au Mississippi*, Paris, 1884, p. 59):

[49] Rev. Israel L. Butt, *History of African Methodism in Virginia: or Four Decades in the Old Dominion* (Hampton, Va., 1908), n.p.

[50] Hampton *Southern Workman*, September, 1884.

[51] Richmond *Planet*, March 23, 1895; *Proceedings of the Negro Protective Association*. Jackson Papers; Morton, *Negro in Virginia Politics*, pp. 139–140.

[52] Charles T. O'Ferrall to Senator Francis [actually Thomas] W. Darling, March 21, 189[5]. O'Ferrall Executive Papers, box no. 372 (Virginia State Library, Richmond, Virginia).

[53] Charles A. Johnson, *A Narrative History of Wise County, Virginia* (Kingsport, Tenn., 1938), pp. 293–295.

[54] Edward A. Freeman, *Some Impressions of the United States* (New York, 1883), p. 148.

. . . there is not a white man in America who would stoop so low as to share his table with a Negro. A black man may be a millionaire but he will never be received in a suitable hotel. At the theater he is often in a separate place. White servants refuse him their service; and strange as it may seem, Negroes themselves do not voluntarily serve their fellowmen.[55]

James Lord Bryce, astute British critic of American institutions, found almost no social mixing of the races even in the North. And unlike Virginia's Lewis H. Blair,[56] he did not exclude Washington, D. C.

Except on the Pacific coast, a negro man never sits down to dinner with a white man in a railway refreshment room. You never encounter him at a private party. He is not received in a hotel of the better sort, no matter how rich he may be. He will probably be refused a glass of soda water at a drug store. He is not shaved in a place frequented by white men, not even by a barber of his own color. He worships in a church of his own. No white woman would dream of receiving his addresses. Nor does it make any difference that he is three parts or seven parts white, if the stain of colour can still be discerned. Kindly condescension is the best he can look for, accompanied by equality of access to a business or profession. Social equality is utterly out of reach.[57]

Another English visitor, William Saunders, found in Virginia that white and black no longer met together in Good

Templar Lodges, "as they formerly did"[58] (presumably during Military Reconstruction). Saunders continued:

I never saw white and coloured men in friendly conversation, and so great is the separation that not in a single instance did I find white and colored children playing together. As fellow workmen, and as master and servant, the two races get on well, but socially there seems to be an impassable barrier between them.[59]

An anonymous English visitor wrote:

. . . the color line in social matters is not likely ever to be broken through. A gradually diminishing minority [sic] is not likely to wrest a privilege from a ruling and increasing majority, the concession of which that same majority now looks on as a calamity worse than death itself.[60]

The Virginia scholar, Philip Alexander Bruce, observed that,

. . . intercourse between the children of the two races [such as was common and accepted in slavery days] is rarely observed now, because the white people, as a rule, are strict in forbidding theirs to turn to such society for diversion. They are induced to do this, primarily, by antipathy of race that makes them careful to preserve the barriers between the negroes and themselves . . . which, they believe, can only be done by keeping the two races as far apart socially as possible.[61]

No wonder that W. E. B. DuBois declared in a social study of Negro life in Farmville, in 1897, that the Negroes there resorted to "group life," having their own churches, organizations, and social life,

---

[55] Translated by and quoted in Evans James Bonaparte, "The Negro in the Writings of French and British Travelers to the United States, 1877–1900," Unpublished M.A. Thesis (Howard University, 1948), p. 37.

[56] Blair, *Prosperity of the South Dependent Upon the Elevation of the Negro*, pp. 60–61.

[57] James Bryce, *The American Commonwealth* (New York and London, 1895, third edition), II, pp. 503–504.

[58] William Saunders, *Through the Light Continent: or the United States in 1877–8* (London, Paris, and New York, 1879), p. 78.

[59] *Ibid.*, pp. 78–79.

[60] Anonymous, "A Social Study of Our Oldest Colony," *Littell's Living Age*, CLXI (1884), 370.

[61] Philip Alexander Bruce, *The Plantation Negro as a Freeman* (New York and London, 1889), p. 52.

and mixed with the whites only in the economic area![62]

When he was relegated to the Jim Crow car by statute in 1900 and disfranchised by the new constitution in 1902, the Virginia Negro lost most of what he had gained since 1865 except his legal freedom and the right to a minimum of public education. Thus, the beginning of the new century marked the birth of a

[62] W. E. B. DuBois, "The Negroes of Farmville, Virginia: A Social Study," *Bulletin of the Department of Labor*, III (1898), 34.

new era in race relations which would see the perfection of the code of racial discrimination and segregation. But in the world of social acceptance at hotels, inns, restaurants, bars, theatres, and other places of amusement, and in the homes and other private circles of the white man, the Virginia Negro had gained nothing which he could lose; for in those areas, by 1900, he stood in essentially the same place and in the same relation to the white man in which he had stood in 1865.

Joel Williamson: THE SEPARATION OF THE RACES

A more general challenge to the Woodward thesis appeared in 1965 in After Slavery: The Negro in South Carolina During Reconstruction, 1861–1877. *The focus of this study was on Reconstruction in South Carolina, while the Woodward thesis was more concerned with later developments in the South at large. Nevertheless, it argued that a relatively rigid pattern of de facto, rather than legal, segregation existed in one Southern state soon after emancipation and persisted through Reconstruction. The core of this argument is contained in the chapter below. The author is an Associate Professor of History at the University of North Carolina, Chapel Hill.*

THE PHYSICAL separation of the races was the most revolutionary change in relations between whites and Negroes in South Carolina during Reconstruction. . . .

During the spring and summer of 1865, as the centripetal force of slavery melted rapidly away, each race clearly tended to disassociate itself from the other. The trend was evident in every phase of human endeavor: agriculture, business, occupations, schools and churches, in every aspect of social intercourse and politics. As early as July of 1865, a Bostonian in

Charleston reported that "the worst sign here . . . is the growth of a bitter and hostile spirit between blacks and whites — a gap opening between the races which, it would seem may at some time result seriously."[1] Well before the end of Reconstruction, separation had crystallized into a comprehensive pattern which, in its essence, remained unaltered until the middle of the twentieth century.

There is no clear, concise answer to the question of why separation occurred. Certainly, it was not simply a response

[1] *New York Times,* July 11, 1865.

From Joel Williamson, *After Slavery: The Negro in South Carolina During Reconstruction, 1861–1877* (1965), pp. 274–99. Reprinted by permission of the University of North Carolina Press.

of Negroes to the prejudiced fiat of dominant whites; nor was it a totally rationalized reaction on the part of either race. Actually, articulate whites and Negroes seldom attempted to explain their behavior. Yet, the philosophies and attitudes each race adopted toward the other lend a certain rationality to separation, and, if we are always mindful that this analysis presumes a unity which they never expressed, can be applied to promote an understanding of the phenomenon.

For the native white community, separation was a means of avoiding or minimizing problems which, they felt, would inevitably arise from the inherent inferiority of the Negro, problems which the North, in eradicating slavery and disallowing the Black Code, would not allow them to control by overt political means. In this limited sense, segregation was a substitute for slavery.

Thus, first, total separation was essential to racial purity, and racial purity was necessary to the preservation of a superior civilization which the whites had labored so arduously to construct, and suffered a long and bloody war to defend. After the war, that civilization was embattled, but not necessarily lost. Unguarded association with an inferior caste would obviously endanger white culture. In this view, children were peculiarly susceptible to damage. "Don't imagine that I allow my children to be with negroes out of my presence," wrote the mistress of a lowcountry plantation in 1868, "on one occasion only have they been so with my knowledge."[2] Even the Negro wet nurse, that quintessence of maternalism upon which the slave period paternalist so often turned his case, emerged as the incubus of Southern in-

fancy. "We gave our infants to the black wenches to suckle," lamented an elderly white, "and thus poisoned the blood of our children, and made them *cowards* . . . the Character of the people of the state was ruined by slavery and it will take 500 years, if not longer, by the infusion of new blood to eradicate the hereditary vices imbibed with the blood (milk is blood) of black wet nurses."[3] Adults, of course, were not immune to racial contamination. Casual associations across the color line might lead to serious ones and to the total pollution of the superior race. Particularly might this be so of the poor, the ignorant, and the feeble-minded, but even the aristocracy had to be watched. Shortly after Redemption, an anonymous Carolinian was incensed at a rumor that Wade Hampton had dined at a table with Negroes in the home of the president of Claflin, the leading Negro university in the state. "Who shall say where it will stop?" he warned. "Will not dining lead to dancing, to social equality, to miscegenation, to mexicanization and to general damnation."[4]

Separation also facilitated the subordination of the inferior race by constantly reminding the Negro that he lived in a world in which the white man was dominant, and in which the non-white was steadfastly denied access to the higher caste. Further, the impression of Negro inferiority would be constantly reinforced by relegating the baser element, whenever possible, to the use of inferior facilities. The sheer totality of the dis-

[2] Mrs. A. J. Gonzales to her mother, May 3, 1868, Elliott-Gonzales Papers.

[3] C. W. Moise to F. W. Dawson, September 15, 1885, F. W. Dawson Papers. See also: A. L. Taveau to William Aiken, April 24, 1865, A. L. Taveau Papers.

[4] Anonymous Ms, n.d., South Carolina Reconstruction Papers. This document was probably found among the papers of Martin Witherspoon Gary. The text indicates that it was written shortly after Redemption.

play alone might well serve to convince members of the lower caste that such, indeed, was in the natural order of things.

Many whites had envisioned the early elimination of the freedman from the Southern scene, and many had eagerly anticipated this event. In time, however, it became evident to all that the Negro would be neither dissolved nor transported to Africa. In a sense, separation was a means of securing the quasi elimination of Negroes at home. It was, perhaps, a more satisfactory solution than their demise or emigration, since it might produce many of the benefits of their disappearance without losing an advantageous, indeed, a necessary supply of labor.

Finally, separation was a logical solution to the problem posed by the widespread conviction that the races were inherently incompatible outside of the master-slave relationship. If the white man could not exist in contentment in the proximity of Negroes, then partial satisfaction might be achieved by withdrawal from associations with members of the inferior caste. This spirit was evident among some of the wealthier whites who voluntarily dispensed entirely with the services of Negro domestics. Elderly William Heyward, in 1868 still second to none in the ranks of the rice aristocracy, stopped taking his meals at the Charleston Hotel because, as he said, he found "the negro waiters so defiant and so familiar in their attentions." "A part of the satisfaction is," he explained to a friend, "that I am perfectly independent of having negroes about me; if I cannot have them as they used to be, I have no desire to see them except in the field."[5] Planters were often manifesting precisely the same sentiment when they deserted their land

and turned to grain culture, or to the use of immigrant labor. Separation was also a way of avoiding interracial violence. B. O. Duncan and James L. Orr, both native white Republicans, argued against mixing in the public schools because they were convinced that minor irritations between children would generate major altercations between parents of different races. Conceived as a means of avoiding violence, separation, ironically, was subsequently enforced by the use of violence.

The Southern white did not always have a clear reason why racial "mixing" (as they called it) in a given situation was wrong, why the color bar should be leveled in one place and not in another. Nevertheless, he had no difficulty in recognizing a breach of the proprieties when he saw it. A young Carolinian visiting New York in the summer of 1867 was outraged by the degree of mixing he observed there: "I can now say that I have seen the city of cities, and after I have seen it it is nothing but vanity and vexation of spirit. Here you can see the negro all on equal footing with white man. White man walking the street with negro wenches. White man and negro riding to gether. White man and negroes sit in the same seat in church or in a word the negro enjoys the same privileges as the white man. They address each other as Mr and Miss but notwithstanding all this we (the southern boys) say what we please and when we please. . . ."[6]

Contrary to common belief, the separation of the races was not entirely the work of the whites. Suspicious, resentful, and sometimes hateful toward the whites, chafed by white attitudes of superiority, and irritated by individual contacts with

5 William Heyward to James Gregorie, June 4, 1868, Gregorie-Elliott Papers.

6 J. H. Young to J. W. White, August 5, 1867, J. W. White Papers.

supercilious whites, Negroes, too, sought relief in withdrawal from association with the other race. In many instances, the disassociation was complete — that is, many Negroes left the state. During the war, Corporal Simon Crum of the First South Carolina declared his intention of leaving South Carolina after the capitulation because, as he phrased it, "dese yer Secesh will neber be cibilized in my time."[7] For those who could not or would not leave, alternative forms of withdrawal were possible. A major facet in the new pattern of agriculture was the removal of Negro labor from the immediate supervision of white men. As the Negro agriculturalist moved his labor away from the eye of the white man, so also did he move his family and his home. Plantation villages became increasingly rare as Negro landowners and renters either built new houses on their plots or, in a rather graphic symbolic display, laboriously dragged their cabins away from the "Negro street." Negroes in the trades and in domestic service followed similar trends. Furthermore, Negroes chose to withdraw from white-dominated churches, though they were often urged to stay, and they attended racially separated schools in spite of the legal fact that all schools were open to all races. Negroes also tended to withdraw from political association with members of the white community.

Finally, on those few occasions when Negroes entered into polite social situations with whites, Northern as well as Southern, they were often ill at ease. For instance, while driving along a road near Columbia, a planter and his wife met William, "a fine looking light mulatto" who had been their stableboy as a slave. William was driving a buggy and seated

beside him was a young white woman, elegantly attired. The woman was a "Yankee school marm," probably one of the new teachers in Columbia's Negro school. As he passed his late master and mistress, the Negro averted his gaze and did not speak. The following day, he approached the planter and apologized for having been escort to a "white woman." He had met the teacher at a celebration, he explained, and she had insisted on his taking her to see the countryside.[8]

During Reconstruction, the Negro's withdrawal was never a categorical rejection of the white man and his society. In the early days of freedom, it was primarily a reaction against slavery, an attempt to escape the unpleasant associations of his previous condition and the derogatory implications of human bondage. However, as the memory of slavery faded, a more persistent reason for withdrawal emerged. Essentially, it was the Negro's answer to discrimination. Almost invariably, attempts by individual Negroes to establish satisfactory relations across the race line were unsuccessful, and, all too often, the pain of the experience was greater than the reward for having stood for principle. During Reconstruction and afterward, only a few were willing to undergo such pain without the certainty of success. It was much easier, after all, simply to withdraw.

Withdrawal as a solution to the race problem was by no means satisfactory to the Negro leadership. Implicit in the behavior of Negro leaders during Reconstruction was a yearning for complete and unreserved acceptance for members of their race by the white community. However, overtly, and rather politically, they carefully distinguished between "social equality" and what might be ap-

[7] Thomas Wentworth Higginson, *Army Life in a Black Regiment* (Boston, 1890), p. 266.

[8] Sally Elmore Taylor MS Memoir.

propriately termed "public equality." For themselves, they claimed only the latter. "Our race do not demand social equality," declared W. J. Whipper, a member from Beaufort, on the floor of the house of representatives in Columbia. "No law can compel me to put myself on an equality with some white men I know," he continued, and, turning cynically on a native white Republican who had vigorously defended separation, concluded, "but talk about equality and the member imagines he must take you into his arms as he probably would your sister, if she was good looking."[9] Two years later, Martin Delany, a man who expressed pride in his blackness, said much the same thing to a large Charleston audience. "I don't believe in social equality; there is no such thing," he shouted. "If we want to associate with a man, we'll do it, and without laws."[10]

What the Negro leadership did insist upon was public equality, that is, absolute civil and political parity with whites and full and free access to most public facilities. These latter included restaurants, bars, saloons, railway and street cars, shipboard accommodations, the theater, and other such places of public amusement. Once they gained political power, Negro leaders hastened to embody this attitude in legislation. Within a week after the first sitting of the Constitutional Convention of 1868, a Negro delegate introduced a resolution which was eventually included in the state's bill of rights: "Distinction on account of race or color, in any case whatever, shall be prohibited, and all classes of citizens shall enjoy equally all common, public, legal and political privileges."[11] Similarly,

one of the first bills passed by the Republican legislature prohibited licensed businesses from discriminating "between persons, on account of race, color, or previous condition, who shall make lawful application for the benefit of such business, calling or pursuit." Convicted violators were liable to a fine of not less than $1,000 or imprisonment for not less than a year.[12] During the debate on the measure in the house, not a single Negro member spoke against the bill, and only five of the twenty-four votes registered against it were cast by Negroes, while fifty-three of the sixty-one votes which secured its passage were those of Negro legislators.[13]

Negro Congressmen were no less ardent in championing the same cause in Washington, particularly in 1874, when a federal civil rights bill was up for consideration. ". . . is it pretended anywhere," asked Congressman R. B. Elliott, who had only recently been denied service in the restaurant of a railway station in North Carolina on his journey to the capital, "that the evils of which we complain, our exclusion from the public inn, from the saloon and table of the steamboat, from the sleeping-coach on the railway, from the right of sepulture in the public burial-ground, are an exercise of the police power of the State? . . . . Are the colored people to be assimilated to an unwholesome trade or to combustible materials, to be interdicted, to be shut up within prescribed limits?" Several days later, in the same place, Congressman R. H. Cain declared, "We do not want any discrimination to be made. I do not ask any legislation for the colored people of this country that is not applied

---

[9] *New York Times*, August 20, 1868.
[10] *Daily Republican* (Charleston), June 24, 1870.
[11] *Convention Proceedings*, 1868, pp. 72, 353–56, 789–92.

[12] *Statutes at Large*, XIV, 179; see also pp. 337–38, 386–88.
[13] *House Journal* (Special Session, 1868), pp. 218–23; *New York Times*, August 20, 1868.

to the white people of this country. All that we seek is equal laws, equal legislation, and equal rights throughout the length and breadth of this land."[14]

It was upon this emotional, uneven ground that an essentially new color line was drawn. It was established in a kind of racial warfare, of assaults and withdrawals, of attacks and counterattacks. Nevertheless, well before the end of Reconstruction, both forces had been fully engaged and the line was unmistakably formed.

Even before the Radicals came into power in South Carolina in 1868, native whites had already defined a color line in government-supported institutions, on common carriers, in places of public accommodation and amusement, and, of course, in private social organizations. The degree of separation in each of these areas varied. In many instances, obviously, some compromise between expense and the desire for complete separation had to be made. Usually, the compromise involved the division of available facilities in some manner. If this was thought to be inconvenient, Negroes were totally excluded.

Typical was the treatment of Negro and white prisoners in the state penitentiary under the James L. Orr regime. Criminals of both races were confined in the same institution but were quartered in separate cells. Ironically, the racial concepts of white prison officials sometimes redounded to the benefit of Negro inmates. Minor violations of prison rules were punished every Sunday by the offenders being tied closely together, blindfolded, and forced to work their way over a series of obstacles in the prison yard. The chief guard explained that the white offenders were placed in

the most difficult middle positions of the "blind gang" because "they have more intelligence than the colored ones and are better able to understand the rules of the institution."[15]

It is paradoxical that the Negro leadership, once in office, pressed vigorously for an end to separation in privately owned facilities open to the public but they allowed a very distinct separation to prevail in every major governmental facility. The most obvious instance was the schools, but the distinction also stretched into the furthermost reaches of gubernatorial activity. For example, a visitor to the state insane asylum in Columbia in 1874 found that "The Negro female inmates occupy a separate part of the same building" in which the white women were housed.[16]

On the other side, within a month after they had gained the vote, Negroes in South Carolina opened a frontal attack against racial discrimination on common carriers. Typical was their assault on the Charleston Street Car Company. At the time of its inauguration, the facilities of the company consisted of double tracks running the length of the peninsula with a spur branching off near the mid-point. Horse-drawn cars, each manned by a driver and a conductor, ran along the tracks at regular intervals. The cars contained seats in a compartment, and front and rear platforms. Before the cars began to run in December, 1866, the question of the accommodation of Negro passengers was thoroughly canvassed. "Proper arrangements will in due time be made to allow persons of color to avail themselves of the benefits of the railway,"

[14] *Congressional Record*, II, Part 1, 43rd Cong., 1st Sess., 408, 566.

[15] *House Journal* (Special Session, 1868), Appendix A, p. 110.

[16] J. E. Bomar to his children, November 26, 1874, E. E. Bomar Papers. See also: Sally Elmore Taylor MS Memoir.

the management assured the Negro community, but it had not then decided between providing "special cars" for the Negroes as was done in New Orleans, or "assigning to them a portion of the ordinary cars as is more usual in other cities."[17] Negro leaders rejected both alternatives. As a Northerner wrote from Charleston in January, 1867, "Every scheme that could be devised that did not contemplate the promiscuous use of the cars by whites and negroes alike, was scouted by the Negro paper here; and the result is that negroes are now debarred the use of the cars altogether, unless they choose to ride upon the platform."[18]

But here the matter did not rest, as the following press account from the *New York Times* will show:

On Tuesday afternoon, March 27, after the adjournment of the Freedmen's mass meeting in Charleston, S. C., an attempt was made by some of them to test their right to ride in the street car, which is denied them by the rules of the Company. One of them entered a car, and declined to leave it when requested to do so by the conductor, who at the same time informed him of the Company's rules. The conductor, however, insisted that he should at least leave the inside of the car, and finally his friends, who found he was liable to be forcibly ejected if resistance were offered, persuaded him to yield. On its return trip the car was filled at the same place by a crowd of negroes, who rushed into it, to the great discomfort of the white passengers, and although remonstrated with and appealed to by the conductor, declined to go out. The driver then attempted, by direction of the conductor, to throw his car from the track; and failing in this, unhitched his horses and left the car. The negroes attempted to push the car forward,

and threatened personal violence to the conductor, but the arrival of the police and detachments of soldiers caused the negroes to disperse. Other cars were in the meantime entered in the same way, and the negroes, finding the conductors would not permit them to ride, endeavored to interrupt the travel of the cars by placing stones on the track . . .[19]

The military soon restored order, but the Negro community prepared to bring the case before the courts.[20] By early May, Negroes were actually riding in the cars, and, by early June, the military commander, Sickles, had issued an order prohibiting racial discrimination on railroads, horse-cars, and steamboats.[21] Sickles's successor, Canby, continued to enforce the rule.[22]

After the Negro gained political power, the battle against discrimination became more intense and assumed a wider front. The so-called antidiscrimination bill, passed in the summer of 1868, on paper was a most formidable weapon. In essence, it imposed severe penalties upon the owners of public accommodations who were convicted of discrimination. Burden of proof of innocence lay on the accused, and state solicitors (public prosecutors) who failed to prosecute suspected violators were themselves threatened with heavy punishments.

The effect of the new legislation on common carriers was immediate. A Northern teacher returning to Beaufort in the fall of 1868, after a few months' absence in the North, observed a portion of the results:

We took a small steamer from Charleston for Beaufort. Here we found a decided

[17] *Daily Courier* (Charleston), October 15, December 17, 1866.
[18] *New York Times,* January 7, 1867.
[19] *Ibid.,* April 2, 1867.
[20] *Ibid.,* April 20, 1867.
[21] W. E. Martin to B. F. Perry, May 7, 1867 (copy), A. L. Burt Papers.
[22] *New York Times,* August 20, 1868.

change since we went North. Then no colored person was allowed on the upper deck, now there were no restrictions, — there could be none, for a law had been passed in favor of the negroes. They were everywhere, choosing the best staterooms and best seats at the table. Two prominent colored members of the State Legislature were on board with their families. There were also several well-known Southerners, still uncompromising rebels. It was a curious scene and full of signficance. An interesting study to watch the exultant faces of the negroes, and the scowling faces of the rebels . . .[23]

The same legislation applied to railway facilities; and, apparently, it was applied without a great amount of dissent. Adjustment was made easier, perhaps, by the acquisition of some of the railroad companies by Radical politicians within the state, or by Northern capitalists, and by the close understanding which usually prevailed between Republican officeholders and those Conservatives who managed to retain control of their railroads. While formal discrimination was not practiced by railway operators, unofficial racial separation did occur on a large scale. On all of the major lines first- and second-class cars were available. Most Negroes apparently deliberately chose to ride in the more economical second-class accommodations, and virtually all of the whites — particularly white women — took passage on the first-class cars. The separation thus achieved was so nearly complete that the first-class car was often referred to as the "ladies' car."[24] It is highly relevant that the first Jim Crow legislation affecting railroads in South Carolina provided for the separation of the races only in the first-class

cars,[25] because, of course, this was the only place on the railroads where there was any possibility of a significant degree of mixing.

During and after Reconstruction, some Negro passengers on the railroads could afford to and did share first-class accommodations with whites, but even this limited mixing was not welcomed by the mass of whites. For instance, a Northern white woman had an interesting and revealing experience while traveling from Columbia to Charleston via the South Carolina Railroad early in 1871:

I must tell you of a scene I saw in the cars coming from Columbia. . . . After we were all seated a black man entered suitably dressed with black pants, black coat, *no* jewelry, trailing a cane. As he came on a man (white in complexion) rose up quickly and grasped the ebony hand with great impressment, and offered him the seat at his side. The colored representative, for such he was, took the seat close to the other, & they commenced a rapid conversation. My ear was arrested at once by the most painful profanity. It came from the *negro*. This [was] an exercise of his freedom, as a slave he would never have dared to utter a word of the kind.

When the Negro representative was reproved by a fellow passenger who happened to be a well known Presbyterian minister, he "took it quietly, and then went out of the car, into the one, (second class I think they called [it]) in front of us." After the minister debarked, the Negro "came back, took a seat by himself, and behaved as well as any person could."[26] A year later, a lady of the lowcountry complained of her trials on a trip by rail from Charleston to Unionville. "Grabbed snatches of sleep on the

[23] Elizabeth Hyde Botume, *First Days among the Contrabands* (Boston, 1893), pp. 267–69.
[24] *New York Times*, October 19, 1868; *Intelligencer* (Anderson), October 21, 1868.

[25] George Brown Tindall, *South Carolina Negroes, 1877–1900* (Columbia, 1952), p. 301.
[26] M. C. M. Taylor to Jeremiah Wilbur, March 13, 1871, Jeremiah Wilbur Papers.

train on the way in spite of our colored neighbors," she reported to her husband.[27] Thus, until 1898, it is possible to find instances in which individual Negroes rode the rails seated in the same cars with the most aristocratic of whites; but economic and social lines reinforced the color line, and the mixture was never generally and freely made.[28]

In the winter of 1869–1870 and through the summer which followed, a concerted attempt was made by the Negro leadership to win the full acceptance of Negroes into all places of public amusement, eating, drinking, and sleeping. Special provisions for the accommodation of Negroes at public entertainments had been made in antebellum times, but physical separation of the races was invariably the rule. In December, 1868, Charles Minort, a mulatto restaurateur and lesser political figure, nearly provoked a riot in a Columbia theater by presuming to seat his wife and himself in the front row, a section traditionally reserved for tardy white ladies. Presumably, he should have chosen seats among the other Negroes present who "had taken their seats, as has always been the custom, in the rear."[29] Minort yielded to the clamor of the whites in the audience, but, a year later, the Negroes of Charleston instituted judicial proceedings against the manager of the Academy of Music for refusing to mix the races in the boxes of the theater. The management barely succeeded in winning a postponement

but was able to complete the season before the case came to trial.[30]

In the spring of 1870, Negro leaders in Charleston launched an attack against discrimination in restaurants, bars, and saloons. On March 25, for instance, Louis Kenake, accused of violating the anti-discrimination act, was brought before Magistrate T. J. Mackey and put on a bond of one thousand dollars while awaiting trial. Other white restaurant keepers of Charleston united to oppose and test the validity of the act, but, in the week which followed, at least six additional charges were lodged against operators of such businesses.[31] The assault was not confined to Charleston, and demonstrations by Radical politicians were frequent during the campaign of 1870. In April, a Laurens woman wrote to her son in Missouri that "On Monday the yankees & some negroes went to Hayne Williams' and asked for drink, which 'Ward' refused them, that is, to drink at the gentlemans bar. They quietly marched him off to jail, & locked the doors, putting the keys in their pockets. The family are all at Spartanburg, we look for H. Williams to night, and I am afraid of a fuss, for he is a great bully."[32] In the same month, during a Radical meeting in Lancaster, a Negro was refused service in a local bar with the comment that no "nigger" could buy a drink there. Lucius Wimbush, a Negro senator, hearing of the incident, went to the bar, ordered a drink, and was refused. He immediately had the barkeeper arrested and placed under bail.[33] Strangely, not all such suits were against whites. "1st case under Civil

[27] Margaret Grimball to John B. Grimball, July 3, 1872, J. B. Grimball Papers.

[28] Negro leaders in this period experienced more difficulty in winning admission to first-class cars in other states. For instance, in December, 1869, three Carolina Negroes sued the Richmond and Danville Railroad for ejecting them from the first-class cars of that Virginia line. *Horry News* (Conway), December 24, 1869.

[29] *New York Times*, December 25, 1868.

[30] *Ibid.*, January 25, 1870.

[31] *Daily Republican* (Charleston), March 26, 28, 29; April 2, 1870.

[32] Mrs. J. W. Motte to Robert Motte, April 27, 1870, Lalla Pelot Papers.

[33] *Daily Republican* (Charleston), April 13, 1870.

Rights Bill today," a Greenville merchant noted in his diary in August, "negro indicts Henry Gantt [a Negro and well-known local barber] for not shaving him where he shaves white persons—— What is to come from it no one knows."[34]

Negroes were also ambitious to open sleeping accommodations to their race. In the summer of 1868, as the first Negro legislators gathered in Columbia, native whites had been extremely apprehensive that they would attempt to occupy rooms in the city's hotels. Even *The Nation,* which had applauded the opening of common carriers to both races, declared that hotels were another and "delicate" matter, where separation was everywhere observed.[35] The white community was vastly relieved to find that no such invasion was attempted, one up-country newspaper having sent a special correspondent to Columbia to ascertain the fact.[36] Nevertheless, when Negro legislators debated the antidiscrimination bill early in the session, they made it very clear that hotels were included. William E. Johnson, the African Methodist Minister then representing Sumter County in the statehouse, noting that the management of Nickerson's Hotel was concerned lest Negroes apply for rooms, declared that if he found private accommodations filled he would want to know that this resort was open to him. George Lee, a Negro member from Berkeley, observed that a group of junketing legislators had recently failed to find lodging in Greenville and that this law was desired to prevent that sort of occurrence. "Equal and exact justice to all," he de-

manded, ". . . it is what we must have."[37] Negroes were subsequently allowed to attend meetings in Columbia hotels, but it is apparent that none were ever given lodging.

Negroes also decried the fact that places of permanent rest occupied by whites, as well as those of a more temporary variety, were denied to their race. For instance, S. G. W. Dill, the native white Radical who was assassinated in Kershaw in the summer of 1868, and Nestor Peavy, his Negro guard who was killed in the same assault, were buried in racially separated cemeteries.[38]

Thus, from 1868 until 1889, when the antidiscrimination law was repealed, Negroes in South Carolina could legally use all public facilities which were open to whites. However, in actual practice, they seldom chose to do so. "The naturally docile negro makes no effort at unnecessary self-assertion," a Northern visitor in Charleston explained in 1870, "unless under the immediate instigation of some dangerous *friends* belonging to the other race, who undertake to manage his destiny."[39] This particular reporter was certainly prejudiced against the race; but four years later another Northern observer congratulated the Negroes of South Carolina on the "moderation and good sense" which they exhibited in their "intercourse with the whites." He concluded, "They seldom intrude themselves into places frequented by the whites, and considering that in South Carolina they have a voting majority of some thirty thousand and control the entire State

---

[34] William L. Mauldin MS Diary, entry for August 22, 1870.

[35] *The Nation,* VII, No. 164 (August 20, 1868), 142.

[36] *Intelligencer* (Anderson), August 26, 1868; *New York Times,* July 12, 1868.

[37] *New York Times,* August 20, 1868.

[38] Thomas J. Kirkland and Robert M. Kennedy, *Historic Camden,* Part Two (Columbia, 1926), p. 202.

[39] N. S. Shaler, "An Ex-Southerner in South Carolina," *Atlantic Monthly,* XXVI, No. 153 (July, 1870), 58.

Government, it is somewhat remarkable that they conduct themselves with so much propriety."[40] Indeed, after 1870, even the Negro leadeship hardly seemed inclined to press further their political and legal advantage to end separation. Of the numerous charges lodged under the anti-discrimination law, not a single conviction was ever recorded.[41]

Even when Negroes pressed themselves in upon the prejudice of whites, the latter adjusted by total or partial withdrawal, so that a high degree of separation was always and everywhere maintained.

Some whites responded to the pressure by total withdrawal, that is, by leaving the state entirely. Of course, many of those who left South Carolina did so primarily for economic reasons, but many also departed from purely racial motives. A Winnsboro lawyer and prewar fire-eater revealed the thinking of many emigrants when he asked William Porcher Miles, in April, 1867, how he could live in a land where "Every 'mulatto' is your Equal & every 'Nigger' is your Superior." Pronouncing the Negro majority "revolting," he advised Miles to go to England. ". . . I have no doubt you could succeed & at any rate wd not have as many Negro Clients & negro witnesses to offend yr nostrils as in these USA. I can't conceive of any ones remaining here who can possibly get away — Suppose, it were certain, wh. it is not, that no U S Congress will ever pass a Law requiring that your Daughter & mine shall either marry Negroes or die unmarried. Still the Negro is already superior to them politically

& to their Fathers also, & must ever be so henceforth."[42]

As the prospect of the elevation of Negroes to political power grew increasingly imminent, restlessness among white Carolinians rose. Joseph Le Conte, nationally famous scientist and a professor at the University of South Carolina, bespoke the minds of many of his colleagues in the fall of 1867. "The prostration of every interest in the Southern States first by the war, & then by the prospect of Negro supremacy, is so great that every one is at least making inquiries in anticipation of being compelled to leave for more favored regions," he wrote to a fellow academician at Yale. "If the present program is carried out it is quite certain that living in these states is simply impossible."[43] Once the Negro was in power, the flood of white emigration swelled. "Better make terms with the Wild Comanches," wrote one exiled Carolinian from the tangles of western Arkansas in 1872, "than hourds of Radicals . . ."[44]

Of course, not every white Carolinian was able to leave the state, but even among those who remained there was a strong current of sentiment for emigration. "I shd. be better satisfied to live and raise my children in a 'white man's country;' and will do so if I can," declared one Baptist clergyman on the eve of the ratification of the Constitution of 1868.[45]

For those who did remain there were lesser degrees of withdrawal. In the one area in which the Negro gained a definite ascendency, politics, a large number of whites simply refused to recognize his

[40] *New York Times,* July 4, 1874. The pattern of separation was also impervious to any effects from the Civil Rights Act of 1875.

[41] Tindall, *South Carolina Negroes,* pp. 292–93, citing the Charleston *News and Courier,* November 5, 1883.

[42] G. I. C. to W. P. Miles, April 13, 1867, W. P. Miles Papers.

[43] Joseph Le Conte to W. D. Whitney, November 28, 1867, W. D. Whitney Papers.

[44] Victor W. Johns to F. W. McMaster, January 9, 1872, F. W. McMaster Papers.

[45] Basil Manly, Jr., to Charles Manly, April 15, 1868, Basil Manly, Jr., Letters and Letterbook.

dominance beyond a necessary, minimal level. In 1870, and in the two state-wide elections which followed, more than ten thousand white voters actually abstained from voting because both regular and "reform" tickets recognized the political existence of the Negro. "They don't like to give up the dead issues of the past," explained a Bishopville farmer to a Virginian, "and are apprehensive that their acknowledgement of the Negroe's Civil and political equality will lead to social leveling."[46] One of those who refused to vote gave as his reason the statement that: "I wish no affiliation with niggers & a platform acknowledging the right of the negro to vote & hold office simply discourages the efforts of the Northern Democracy. The privilege may be *allowed the negro at this time to vote & c* but it is certainly not a right."[47] Many of those who voted the reform ticket did so only with grave reservations. While honoring "Hampton, Butler, Kershaw & gentlemen of that character" for their "courage and endurance" in attempting to fashion a program in 1870, a Charleston aristocrat asserted that: "Some of us have been unable to bring ourselves to admit the right to give the negro these rights of citizenship & are therefore unable to join in the canvas, but even we who are, possibly of this mistaken conscientious opinion, will vote the Reform Union (as it is called) candidates & rejoice at their success."[48] Even those who actively campaigned as Reformers, while embracing the Negro politically, kept him at arm's length socially. Attending a Reform speaking and barbecue in 1870, the Rev-

erend Cornish noted that the participants dined at two tables, "the negroes at one & the whites at another."[49]

After Negroes were firmly entrenched in official positions in government, native whites evinced a distinct tendency to refrain from associations which recognized the authority of Negro officers over white citizens. For instance, in the heavily Negro county of Abbeville, in 1870, a distressed guardian asked one of the magistrates, who happened to be a Democrat, to dispatch a constable to return an orphan girl stolen away from his house. "When you send for Laura," he begged, "please send a white man, as she is a white girl under my charge, and I would not like to subject her to the mortification of being brought back by a colored man. Besides that I would be censured by the community as they would know nothing of the circumstances of the case."[50] Very often, avoiding communication with Negro officeholders was an easy matter for the whites. In the predominantly white counties, Conservatives were always able to retain some offices. In the counties where the Negroes were heavily in the majority, there were usually white Republicans in office through whom the local whites might and did conduct their business with the government. Contrary to tradition, when carpetbaggers and scalawags were actually in office, and there was every prospect that they would remain so throughout the foreseeable future, the white community did not think them all nearly so odious personally as subsequent reports suggested. Even in the middle counties, where the native Negro leadership predominated and scalawags did

[46] J. M. Dennis to J. Y. Harris, May 21, 1870, J. Y. Harris Papers.
[47] T. P. Bailey to R. H. McKie, May 12, 1870, R. H. McKie Papers.
[48] W. G. De Saussure to W. P. Miles, September 21, 1870, W. P. Miles Papers. The writer was mistaken in including Hampton in this group.

[49] J. H. Cornish MS Diary, entry for September 3, 1870.
[50] E. F. Powers to R. R. Hemphill, May 21, 1870, Hemphill Papers.

tend to be political opportunists, native whites still found means of avoiding contacts with Republican officers which, to them, would have been humiliating. A typical resort was that of the white citizens of Camden who arranged for the introduction of a bill in the legislature by a conservative representative from the white county of Lancaster because, as a Camdenite indicated, "our Representatives were coloured, and scalawags."[51]

Withdrawal was also the means by which native whites combatted attempts by Republican officials to end separation in institutions supported by the government. The withdrawal of native whites from the University and the State School for the Deaf and Blind at the prospect of Negro admissions are illustrations of white determination either to maintain separation or to dispense with the services afforded by related state institutions. If the Radicals had attempted to end separation in the common schools, it is virtually certain that the whites would have removed their children from these schools too. As one post-Redemption proponent of universal education argued, separation was essential to academic progress. Only by this means, he explained to Governor Hampton, could it be achieved "without any danger of social equality — *and this is the great bug bear.*"[52] Doubtless, it was the threat of withdrawal by the whites which dissuaded the Radical leadership from further attempts to end separation in institutions over which they had, by political means, absolute control.

Whites also refused to engage in normal civic activities in which the color line was not distinctly drawn. Thus, native whites chose not to join militia companies in which Negroes participated and were reported to be extremely apprehensive of being forced to undergo the "humiliation" of joining a mixed company.[53] Too, whites were reluctant to sit with Negroes in the jury box. An elderly Spartanburg farmer verbalized his feelings on this point in the summer of 1869: "When I go to court & see negroes on the jury & on the stand for witnesses it makes me glad that I am so near the end of my race to sit on a jury with them I dont intend to do it we have a law that exempt a man at 65 & I take the advantage of it."[54] This kind of withdrawal often reached odd extremes. In the spring of 1870, at the peak of the Negro leadership's drive for admission to privately owned public accommodations, the white Democrats of the Charleston Fire Department refused to decorate their engines and join in the annual parade because Negro fire companies were being allowed to march in the procession.[55]

This general withdrawal of whites from participation in civil affairs resulted in a tendency within the white community to govern itself outside of the official system. As Reconstruction progressed, this peculiar form of dyarchy approached its logical culmination. In its last days, the Tax Union came very close to the establishment of a separate government within the state when it considered collecting a ten-mill tax from its members and supervising its expenditure, thus depriving the incumbent Radicals of the staff of political life.[56] A year later, during the period of the dual government, a similar plan was actually implemented while the Hampton regime governed the

51 R. A. Bonney to Dock Bonney, August 2, 1868, E. W. Bonney Papers.
52 Anonymous to Wade Hampton, November 13, 1877, Freedmen File.
53 *New York Times*, May 24, 1867.
54 Edward Lipscomb to Smith Lipscomb, June 30, 1869, Edward Lipscomb Papers.
55 *Daily Republican* (Charleston), April 30, 1870.
56 *Intelligencer* (Anderson), December 2, 1875.

whites and the Chamberlain government served, virtually, a Negro constituency.

Native whites also tended to withdraw from public places where the color line could not be firmly fixed and the Negro could easily assert his equality. "The whites have, to a great extent — greater than ever before — yielded the streets to the negroes," wrote a Columbian on Christmas Day, 1868.[57] Similarly, in Charleston, in the late spring of 1866, a young aristocrat noted that the battery with its music and strollers had been yielded to the ladies and gentlemen of non-noble lineage on Saturdays, and by all whites to the Negroes on Sundays. On Saturdays, he declared, "the battery is quite full of gentlemen and ladies but it is not much patronized by the elite. . . . On Sunday afternoon the ethiops spread themselves on the Battery."[58]

The same reaction was manifested by the whites wherever the Negro leadership succeeded by legal means in ending separation. For instance, when Negroes won admission to the street cars of Charleston, the whites simply withdrew. "On Sunday I counted five Cars successively near the Battery crowded [with] negroes, with but one white man, the Conductor," wrote a native white in May, 1867. "The ladies are practically excluded."[59] When the Academy of Music was threatened with a discrimination suit in 1870, the white community replied with a counterthreat to withdraw its patronage and thus close the theater.[60] Adjustment which fell short of complete separation remained unsatisfactory to whites. "Even the Theatre is an uncertain pleasure," complained a Charleston

lady in 1873, "no matter how attractive the program, for you know that you may have a negro next to you."[61] Probably many of her contemporaries found the exposure too damaging and stayed home.

The social lives of native whites were, of course, absolutely closed to Negroes. Access to the homes of the whites was gained by Negroes only when they clearly acquiesced in the superior-inferior relationship dictated by the owners, and even then entrance was often denied. "I told him I would never allow negroes to go in it while I owned it," wrote a Laurensville woman, incensed that a man who had bought her former home had rented it to Negroes. In spite of the fact that some Negro domestics lived in quarters behind the houses of their employers, whites were already rejecting Negroes as neighbors. A real estate agent in Aiken in 1871 responded to this sentiment when he refused offers from Negroes for city lots at triple prices because, as he explained to the owner, "purchasers among the whites will not settle among the Negroes, and I am afraid to sell to only a few of the latter."[62] Negroes were also not permitted to join any of the numerous social organizations in which native whites participated. The Patrons of Husbandry (the Grange), waxing strong in the state in the early 1870's, was not only exclusively white in membership, but was accused of widening the racial gap by its attitudes and actions toward Negroes.[63] Of course, such separation had been practiced before, but the exclusion of the Negro in freedom from the social

[57] New York Times, January 2, 1869.
[58] Berkeley Grimball to Elizabeth Grimball, June 10, 1866, J. B. Grimball Papers (Duke).
[59] W. E. Martin to B. F. Perry, May 7, 1867 (copy), A. L. Burt Papers.
[60] New York Times, January 25, 1870.

[61] Eliza M. Smith to W. P. Miles, January 16, 1873, W. P. Miles Papers.
[62] Mrs. Robert Pelot to her husband, March 11, 1866, Lalla Pelot Papers; F. A. Ford to James Conner, November 27, 1871, James Conner Papers.
[63] William A. Law to his wife, August 29, 1874; A History of Spartanburg County, p. 168.

organizations of the whites was not so much tradition as it was deliberate decision. For instance, witness the outrage of an officer of the Donaldsville Lodge of Good Templars at a careless assertion by the Abbeville *Medium* that the Lodge had admitted Negroes to membership. "I want to inform you," he lectured the editors, "that we have no negroes in our Lodge of Good Templars as you stated in your Last paper that we had formed a Lodge of Good Templars Numbering 45 including children & negroes. we don't take negroes in our Lodge. If you Do dont send me any nother number."[64]

The average Northern white residing in South Carolina during Reconstruction was only slightly less inclined than his native white contemporary to enforce racial separation. During the war, of course, Negro troops were organized in separate regiments, bivouacked in separate camps, and, when wounded, housed in separate hospitals.[65] After the war, although still sympathetic to most of the interests of the Negro, many Northern residents continued to draw a very distinct race line. In March, 1867, presumably under the influence of a man who had commanded a Negro brigade, many of the whites on St. Helena moved to establish a separate church from which Negroes would be excluded. Further, two months later when the Negroes of the island met to form a Republican organization, most of the Northern white residents boycotted the meeting, saying they were "going to have a *white* party."[66]

Apparently, at least some of this sentiment carried over into the Constitutional Convention of 1868, because, as a Northern correspondent observed, white delegates occupied the front rows while Negroes filled the seats at the rear of the hall.[67] By 1870, separation also marked the formal social life of the official community in Columbia. Governor Scott, himself, set the precedent. In January, 1869, it was noted that no Negroes attended the traditional annual ball of the governor. The omission caused a great outcry — the loudest of which, incidentally, came from Franklin J. Moses, Jr., the native white speaker of the house who became the next governor of the state on the suffrage of a Negro electorate. Governor Scott responded to the criticism by holding open house every Thursday evening to which all comers were welcomed. It was soon observed, however, that only Negro politicians called at that time.[68]

Informally, there was considerable social intercourse between Negroes and some Northern missionaries and white Radical politicians, Southern as well as Northern in birth. For instance, as revealed through her diary, the Quaker schoolmistress Martha Schofield never thought or acted in any way discriminatory against Negroes as a race.[69] Frank Moses, politically the most successful of the scalawags, after 1868, publicly, repeatedly, and consistently supported unreserved equality for Negroes. Similarly, in Charleston, in 1870, a scandalized aristocrat declared that Mrs. Bowen, the wife of scalawag Congressman Christopher Columbus Bowen and the daughter of a unionist leader in the nullification

64 O. P. Gordon to R. R. Hemphill, June 21, 1874, Hemphill Papers.
65 Emma E. Holmes MS Diary, entry for April 7, 1865; Rupert S. Holland, *Letters and Diary of Laura M. Towne, 1862–1884, Written from the Sea Islands of South Carolina* (Cambridge, 1912), p. 116.
66 Holland, *Letters and Diary of Laura M. Towne*, pp. 177–78, 182.

67 *New York Times*, January 27, 1868.
68 *Ibid.*, February 6, 1869; January 25, 1870; Charleston *Daily Republican*, February 19, 1870.
69 Martha Schofield MS Diary, *passim*.

controversy in the 1830's, "is reported to receive negro visitors. . . . thank Heaven," he added gratefully, "that Mr. Petigru cannot see her degradation . . ."[70] Perhaps in time the quantity of interchange increased slightly. A Northern observer, visiting the state in 1874, noted that the "shoddy" Northerners living in South Carolina "hob nob" with the blacks in the bars and have them at home and that "at least two politicians of Charleston have married colored wives . . ."[71] Taken at large, however, most white Republicans apparently accepted "public equality" for Negroes; but only a few broadened their toleration to accept Negroes into their social activities.

Separation is, of course, a relative term. It was obviously not possible for Negroes and whites to withdraw entirely from association with each other. If intimate contact led to irritation and violence, it also led to warm personal friendships — often with the superior-inferior, paternal bias, but no less real for all of that. Cordiality could and did breach the barrier of race; yet the fact remained that it was difficult to establish a human bond across the color chasm and, once established, the tie had to be assiduously maintained against the constant erosion induced by a thousand and one external forces of social pressure.

That there was sometimes tenderness between individuals of different races is abundantly evident. On the Elmore plantation near Columbia, in the fall of 1865, the young white master was nightly importuned by the Negro children to get out his fiddle and play. Frequently he did so, the dozen or so Negro boys and girls dancing around the fire, begging for more after the fiddler had exhausted him-

self in a two-hour concert.[72] The concern of many late masters for their ex-slaves was matched by the interest of individual Negroes in the welfare of their recent owners. A freedman seeking relief for a white family from a Bureau officer explained his motivation: "I used to belong to one branch of that family, and so I takes an interest in 'em."[73] Occasionally, ex-slaveowners retained the friendship and assistance of their erstwhile bondsmen when all others had deserted them. Thus, in the summer of 1873, in an area of Chester county where alleged Klansmen had been active two years previously, planter Robert Hemphill noted the death of a neighbor, John McCluken. "I called one morning & found him dead & the dogs in bed with him," he reported. "Strange to say there was no white person ever called to see him. The negroes were the only persons who gave him any attention at all."[74]

Sometimes, intimacy became miscegenation. The census reports are uncertain witnesses and contemporaries are typically mute on the point; but scattered references suggest that racial interbreeding was markedly less common after emancipation than before. "Miscegenation between white men and negro women diminished under the new order of things," a Bureau officer later wrote. "Emancipation broke up the close family contact in which slavery held the two races, and, moreover young gentlemen did not want mulatto children sworn to them at a cost of three hundred dollars apiece. In short, the new relations of the two stocks tended to separation rather

[70] W. G. De Saussure to W. P. Miles, September 21, 1870, W. P. Miles Papers.
[71] New York Times, July 9, 1874.

[72] Grace B. Elmore MS Diary, entry for October 1, 1865.
[73] James H. Croushore and David M. Potter (eds.), John William De Forest, A Union Officer in the Reconstruction (New Haven, 1948), p. 65.
[74] R. N. Hemphill to W. R. Hemphill [Summer], 1873, Hemphill Papers.

than to fusion."[75] A Northern traveler visiting the state in 1870 concurred: "From all I could see and learn, there are far fewer half-breed children born now than before the Rebellion. There seems, indeed, a chance that the production of original half-breeds may be almost done away with. . . ."[76]

Legal, moral, and social pressures exercised by the white community upon its members, as well as the physical separation of the races suggest that these were valid observations. The Black Code pointedly declared that "Marriage between a white person and a person of color shall be illegal and void," and when the code was revised in 1866 this portion emphatically remained in force.[77] Children born of Negro mothers and white fathers, so recently especially prized for their pecuniary value, became simply illegitimate issue and a liability to the community. In addition, the laws of bastardy came to be applied against the fathers of mulatto children. Perhaps most important was the fact that, in the minds of the native whites, children of mixed blood personified the adulteration of the superior race and embodied in living form the failure of Southern civilization. Many whites, turned to soul-searching by their defeat, fixed upon miscegenation as their great sin. "It does seem strange that so lovely a climate, and country, with a people in every way superior to the Yankees, should be overrun and destroyed by them," wrote a rice aristocrat in 1868. "But I believe that God has ordered it all, and I am firmly of opinion with Ariel that it is the judgement of the Almighty because the human and brute blood have mingled to the degree it has in the slave states. Was it not so in the French and

British Islands and see what has become of them."[78]

Just as complete separation of the races was physically impossible, there was little possibility that miscegenation might entirely cease. One does not have to travel far into contemporary sources to discover instances in which white men had children by Negro women. In 1867, a low-country planter, accused of fathering the mulatto child of his Negro house servant, wrote plaintively to his mother: "This child was begotten during my absence in Charlotte & Charleston, from the middle of December until nearly the middle of January, & the Father of it was seen night after night in Emma's house, this I heard on my return, but as it was no concern of mine I did not give it a thought. She was *free,* the Mother of 5 Children & could have a dozen lovers if she liked. I had no control over her virtue."[79] In 1874, a planter on the Cooper River in St. John's noted the existence of circumstances on his plantation which might have led to similar results. "Found a white man staying with one of the colored people on the place," ran the laconic note in his journal. "He being engaged in rebuilding Mayrents Bridge."[80] Some of these liaisons were of prolonged duration. In 1870, Maria Middleton, a Negro woman, brought suit against a Pineville physician for failure to support her three children which he had allegedly fathered. Strangely, the defendant's lawyer did not deny the paternity, but sought dismissal on the plea that the plaintiff had no legal grounds for suit.[81]

Once in power, the Radicals hastened

[75] Croushore and Potter, *A Union Officer,* p. 132.
[76] Shaler, *Atlantic Monthly,* XXVI, p. 57.
[77] *Statutes at Large,* XII, 270, 366[29]–366[30].

[78] William Heyward to James Gregorie, January 12, 1868, Gregorie-Elliott Papers.
[79] T. R. S. Elliott to his mother, October 20, 1867, T. R. S. Elliott Papers.
[80] Keating S. Ball MS Plantation Journal, entry for February 5, 1874.
[81] *Daily Republican* (Charleston), June 7, 1870.

to repeal the prohibition against inter-racial marriage. Thereafter, informal arrangements were sometimes legalized. In the spring of 1869, a reporter stated that three such marriages had occurred within the state — a Massachusetts man had married a Beaufort mulatto woman, and two white women had married Negro men.[82] In 1872, the legislature explicitly recognized interracial unions by declaring that the "children of white fathers and negro mothers may inherit from the father if he did not marry another woman but continued to live with their mother."[83]

There were a surprisingly large number of cases in which white women gave birth to children by Negro fathers. During his stay in Greenville, Bureau officer John De Forest heard of two such births and noted other instances in which white women were supported by Negro men. Such situations, he believed, were largely the result of the loss of husbands and fathers in the war and the destitution of the country generally.[84] In 1866, in neighboring Pickens District, a case came into the courts in which Sally Calhoun, "a white woman of low birth," and a Negro man were brought to trial for the murder of their child. Ironically, the Negro was freed, though obviously implicated, and the woman was convicted and imprisoned.[85] Apparently, some of these liaisons were far from casual as a Spartanburg farmer rather painfully suggested to his brother in Alabama: "My dear Brother as you have made several Enquiries of me and desiring me to answer them I will attempt and endeavor to do So to the best information that I have on the Various Subjects alluded to by you the first

Interrogatory is Relative to John H. Lipscomb's daughter haveing Negro Children, I am forced to answer in the affirmative . . . no doubt but she has had two; and no hopes of her Stopping. . . ."[86]

By the end of Reconstruction, Negroes had won the legal right to enjoy, along with whites, accommodations in all public places. In reality, however, they seldom did so. On the opposite side of the racial frontier, the pattern of separation was fixed in the minds of the whites almost simultaneously with the emancipation of the Negro. By 1868, the physical color line had, for the most part, already crystallized. During the Republican regime, it was breached only in minor ways. Once the whites regained political power, there was little need to establish legally a separation which already existed in fact. Moreover, to have done so would have been contrary to federal civil rights legislation and would have given needless offense to influential elements in the North. Finally, retention of the act had a certain propaganda value for use against liberals in the North and against Republican politicians at home. Again and again, the dead letter of the law was held up as exhibit "A" in South Carolina's case that she was being fair to the Negro in the Hampton tradition. After the federal statute was vitiated in the courts, after racial liberalism had become all but extinct in the North, and as the Negro was totally disfranchised in South Carolina, the white community was ready and able to close the few gaps which did exist in the color line, and to codify a social order which custom had already decreed.

Ultimately, the physical separation of the races is the least important portion of the story. The real separation was not

---

[82] *New York Times,* May 24, 1869.
[83] *Statutes at Large,* XIII, 62–63.
[84] Croushore and Potter, *A Union Officer,* p. 138.
[85] *House Journal* (Special Session, 1868), Appendix A, pp. 134–35. See also: *New York Times,* November 9, 1866.

[86] Edward Lipscomb to Smith Lipscomb, June 19, 1874, Lipscomb Family Papers.

that duo-chromatic order that prevailed on streetcars and trains, or in restaurants, saloons, and cemeteries. The real color line lived in the minds of individuals of each race, and it had achieved full growth even before freedom for the Negro was born. Physical separation merely symbolized and reinforced mental separation. It is true that vigorous assaults by one side or the other forced the enemy to yield his forward trenches and to alter slightly the precise line of the color front. It is also true that material changes in post-Reconstruction Southern society pushed the trenches into areas which had not existed before. This often gave the illusion of basic change, of a breakthrough by the dominant whites in the war of races, whereas, actually, it merely represented the extension of the old attitudinal conflict onto new ground, only to bring with it the stalemate that marked the struggle elsewhere. Viewed in relation to the total geography of race relations, the frontier hardly changed; and the rigidity of the physical situation, set as it was like a mosaic in black and white, itself suggested the intransigence of spirit which lay behind it. Well before the end of Reconstruction, this mental pattern was fixed; the heartland of racial exclusiveness remained inviolate; and South Carolina had become, in reality, two communities — one white and the other Negro.

II. HISTORICAL AND PSYCHOLOGICAL ROOTS OF SEGREGATION

C. Vann Woodward: WHY NEGROES WERE SEGREGATED
IN THE NEW SOUTH

In 1951, in Origins of the New South, *Professor Woodward outlined the process by which the Negro freedman became the object of discrimination and segregation. After Reconstruction, he indicated, race relations were still relatively fluid in the South. But industrialism and the development of a new economic order brought the white masses into direct competition with Negro workers, and as the laboring whites gained political power they imposed their harsh code of race relations upon the Negroes. Above all, the author seems to say, it was the demise of upper-class paternalism in Southern politics and the rise of white democracy which caused the degradation and segregation of the Negro.*

IN THE working out of a new code of civil rights and social status for the freedman — in the definition of the Negro's "place" — Reconstruction had been only an interruption, the importance of which varied from state to state, but which was nowhere decisive. The transition from slavery to caste as a system of controlling race relations went forward gradually and tediously. Slavery had been vastly more than a labor system, and the gap that its removal left in manners, mores, and ritual of behavior could not be filled overnight. The so-called "Black Codes" were soon overthrown, as were the laws imported by the Carpetbaggers. Redemption and Hayes's policy of *laissez faire* left the code to be worked out by Southern white men. It has already been pointed out that there was no unity of opinion among them concerning the Negro's political rights. There also existed a roughly comparable division with reference to his civil rights.

Hampton, Lamar, Nicholls, and Redeemers of that type gave their solemn pledges in the Compromise of 1877 to protect the Negro in all his rights. They were probably guilty of less hypocrisy than has been charged. The class they represented had little to fear from the Negro and at the same time considerable to gain for the conservative cause by establishing themselves in a paternalistic relationship as his protector and champion against the upland and lower-class whites. This would better enable them to control his vote (against the same white element), not to mention his labor. In 1877 J. L. M. Curry listened to a debate of the Virginia Assembly in Jefferson's neoclassic capitol. "A negro member," he recorded with evident satisfaction in his diary, "said that he and his race relied

From C. Vann Woodward, *Origins of the New South, 1877–1913* (1951), pp. 209–12. Reprinted by permission of Louisiana State University Press. A paperback edition of this volume was issued in 1966.

for the protection of their rights & liberties, not on the 'poor white trash' but on the 'well-raised' gentlemen."[1] Black-Belt white men were casual about their daily intimacy and easy personal relations with Negroes, an attitude that made upland Southerners uncomfortable and shocked Northerners, even Radical Carpetbaggers. So long as this old leadership retained strong influence, the racial code was considerably less severe than it later became.

In the early years of freedom saloons in Mississippi usually served both whites and blacks at the same bar; many public eating places, "using separate tables, served both races in the same room"; public parks and buildings were still open to both to a great extent; and segregation in common carriers was not at all strict.[2] The most common type of discrimination on railways was the exclusion of Negroes from the first-class, or "ladies' " car. The races were accustomed to sharing the second-class coach. In 1877, however, a South Carolinian wrote that Negroes were "permitted to, and frequently do ride in first-class railway and street railway cars" in his state. This had caused trouble at first but was "now so common as hardly to provoke remark."[3] In 1885 George W. Cable, who was sensitive regarding discrimination, reported that in South Carolina Negroes "ride in the first class cars as a right" and "their

presence excites no comment," while "In Virginia they may ride exactly as white people do and in the same cars."[4] Even the ante-bellum practice of using a common cemetery continued for many years. White papers occasionally "mistered" Negro politicians, if they were "good" politicians, and a Richmond paper affirmed in 1886 that "nobody here objects to sitting in political conventions with negroes. Nobody here objects to serving on juries with negroes."[5] Even the Tillman legislature of 1891 defeated a Jim Crow bill for railway cars.

From the beginning, however, concessions to the harsher code and developing phobias of the hillbillies of the white counties had to be made. There were South Carolinians in numbers who did not share the Charleston *News and Courier*'s feeling that it was "a great deal pleasanter to travel with respectable and well-behaved colored people than with unmannerly and ruffianly white men."

It is one of the paradoxes of Southern history that political democracy for the white man and racial discrimination for the black were often products of the same dynamics. As the Negroes invaded the new mining and industrial towns of the uplands in greater numbers, and the hill-country whites were driven into more frequent and closer association with them, and as the two races were brought into rivalry for subsistence wages in the cotton fields, mines, and wharves, the lower-class white man's demand for Jim Crow laws became more insistent. It took a lot of ritual and Jim Crow to bolster the creed of white supremacy in the bosom of a white man working for a

---

[1] Diary of J. L. M. Curry, January 13, 1877, in Curry Papers.
[2] Wharton, *Negro in Mississippi*, p. 232. The evolution of "caste as a method of social control" is admirably worked out by this author.
[3] Belton O'Neall Townsend, "South Carolina Society," in *Atlantic Monthly*, XXXIX (1877), 676. Commenting in 1879 on the "perfect equality" of races in Southern tramcars, a member of Parliament wrote: "I was, I confess, surprised to see how completely this is the case; even an English Radical is a little taken aback at first," Sir George Campbell, *White and Black* . . . (New York, 1879), p. 195.

[4] Cable, *Silent South*, pp. 85–86. Cable was quoting the Charleston *News and Courier* with regard to South Carolina. The observation on Virginia custom is his own.
[5] Richmond *Dispatch*, October 13, 1886.

black man's wages. The Negro pretty well understood these forces, and his grasp of them was one reason for his growing alliance with the most conservative and politically reactionary class of whites against the insurgent white democracy. A North Carolina Negro wrote: "The best people of the South do not demand this separate car business . . . and, when they do, it is only to cater to those of their race who, in order to get a big man's smile, will elevate them [sic] to place and power." He believed that "this whole thing is but a pandering to the lower instincts of the worst class of whites in the South."[6]

The barriers of racial discrimination mounted in direct ratio with the tide of political democracy among whites. In fact, an increase of Jim Crow laws upon the statute books of a state is almost an accurate index of the decline of the reactionary regimes of the Redeemers and triumph of white democratic movements. Take, for example, the law requiring separate accommodations for the races in trains, said to be "the most typical Southern law." No state[7] enacted such a law for more than twenty years after 1865. Yet in the five years beginning in 1887 one after another adopted some variation of the law: Florida in 1887, Mississippi in 1888, Texas in 1889, Louisiana in 1890, Alabama, Arkansas, Kentucky, and Georgia in 1891. These were the years when

the Farmers' Alliance was first making itself felt in the legislatures of these states. Mississippi, in 1888, was the first state to adopt a law providing for the separation of the races in railway stations, and Georgia, in 1891, the first to adopt the law for streetcars.[8] These laws, though significant in themselves, were often only enactments of codes already in practice. Whether by state law or local law, or by the more pervasive coercion of sovereign white opinion, "the Negro's place" was gradually defined — in the courts, schools, and libraries, in parks, theaters, hotels, and residential districts, in hospitals, insane asylums — everywhere, including on sidewalks and in cemeteries. When complete, the new codes of White Supremacy were vastly more complex than the ante-bellum slave codes or the Black Codes of 1865–1866, and, if anything, they were stronger and more rigidly enforced.

In 1955, in The Strange Career of Jim Crow, *Professor Woodward elaborated significantly upon his earlier description of why Jim Crow came to be. In a key chapter entitled "Capitulation to Racism"* he asserted that during Reconstruction and for some years thereafter Northern liberalism, Southern conservatism, and Southern radicalism checked extreme racism and maintained a comparative plasticity in race relations. In the 1890's, however, each of these elements collapsed. Particularly in the South in that decade, the conservative politicians found themselves unable to*

---

[6] Editorial, *Southland* (Salisbury, N. C.), I (1890), 166–67.

[7] The Tennessee legislature passed an act in 1875 abrogating the common law and releasing common carriers and other public servants from serving anyone they chose not to serve. A Federal circuit court declared this unconstitutional in 1880. An act of 1881 required separate first-class accommodations for Negroes, but left the two races unsegregated in second-class coaches. Stanley J. Folmsbee, "The Origin of the First 'Jim Crow' Law," in *Journal of Southern History,* XV (1949), 235–47.

[8] Franklin Johnson, *Development of State Legislation Concerning the Free Negro* (New York, 1919), pp. 15, 54, 62–207; Gilbert T. Stephenson, *Race Distinctions in American Law* (New York, 1910), pp. 216–17.

* *The Strange Career of Jim Crow* (New York: The Oxford University Press, 1966 edition), pp. 67–109.

cope with the ill effects of a rapidly in-
dustrializing economy. Faced with popular rebellion in a society which they had
long dominated, conservatives took fright
and resorted to racist appeals even as
they counted in for themselves Negro
votes which had not been cast. Economic, social, and political frustrations
thus generated aggressiveness among the
great mass of whites, the Negro became
the scapegoat for these aggressions, and
Northerners permitted it to be so. Confronted with a rising tide of white terror,
many Negroes lost the will to resist and
adopted the tactics of accommodation.
For the Negro, the result of this almost
chance and rather strange concatenation
of economic, political, and psychological
circumstances was disfranchisement, discrimination, and segregation.

It is evident that in 1954 and 1955 Professor Woodward was focusing his schol-
arly talents very sharply upon the problem of how Americans and particularly
Southerners of both races might best
adjust to the new order of race relations.
His stress upon the decline of Northern
liberalism in the rise of racial discrimination in the South indicated the importance of outside pressure in bringing
about a New Reconstruction in the South.
The suggestion that the Negro's own

accommodationist tendencies accelerated
his previous decline argued that the
Negro now must assert himself to rise
into his rights. Southern conservatives
and Southern radicals each had a legitimate tradition of racial moderation to
which they might easily return. In ap-
propriating the concept that frustration
breeds aggression and aggression requires a scapegoat, Professor Woodward
also added, as many historians were doing in that decade, the teachings of social
psychology to his interpretation. Discrimination and segregation hence became the fruit of a lamentable but understandable psychosis, and a psychosis, the
psychiatrists told us, was most curable
when its source was known. Segregation
in the South, then, was decided under
crisis conditions which created in the
mind of the whites a sort of temporary
insanity. The South acted upon a series
of options hastily, made the wrong decisions, and now must correct its error. Finally, the tools for correction are immediately at hand. Laws had often created
segregated situations with the counting
of a legislator's vote; in our own time
legislation could as easily reverse the
process.

Editor's note.

Charles E. Wynes: IN SUMMATION

*In the following selection, Dr. Wynes presented a summary of his
findings on integration and segregation in Virginia, a brief explanation
of how segregation came to be enacted into law in that state, and a
concise evaluation of the effect of his findings on the Woodward thesis.*

From Charles E. Wynes, *Race Relations in Virginia, 1870–1902* (1961), pp. 148–50. Reprinted by
permission of The University Press of Virginia.

MEANWHILE, the Negro had made a small measure of progress in the social realm even as relations on the political scene deteriorated. This created the seeming anomaly of the Negro's gaining socially while he lost politically. But in reality the situation was anomalous only on the surface. Social progress, though severely limited, was determined by the whole people and reflected their attitudes. Political regression was largely the work of both Democratic and Republican party leaders — politicians whose chief aim was to control the vote and who knew that making the Negro the scapegoat of the social ills of the day would appeal to most white voters.

While the Negro was being driven from the polls, he was gaining increasing acceptance of the right to ride the state's railroads in seats of his own choosing. That he did not make commensurate gains in other areas, such as accommodation in hotels, restaurants, and theatres, is at least as much due to the fact that he made no concerted fight for those rights as it is due to any "natural prejudice" by the white man. He won the right to sit where he chose in interstate railroad travel by taking the matter into the Federal courts, and he won increasing acceptance of the right to sit where he chose in intrastate travel by insisting upon the right in great numbers. And never at any time did there develop universal demand that he be relegated to Jim Crow cars. Only a few Democratic newspapers voiced this demand, and there is not sufficient evidence to prove that they spoke for the majority of the people. Meanwhile, the whole issue was obscured by referring to those rights as social rights when they were in reality only civil rights.

All this is not to deny that almost universal prejudice against the Negro did exist. It did. But prejudice did not rule out increasing acceptance, even if that acceptance was granted grudgingly, as it usually was. Neither did prejudice demand disfranchisement nor segregation by statute. Yet it cannot be denied that a highly prejudiced press influenced an already prejudiced white people to accept both as natural, inevitable, and right. As a political issue, the Negro was too tempting for the politicians to let alone. When the issue of the Negro promised to suit their ends, they used it. When a reduced electorate appeared to be advantageous, they disfranchised him. The Virginia legislators who disfranchised the Negro and segregated him by statute were *not* led by representatives of that class of white people who competed directly with the Negro economically and who were more likely to be thrown with him socially. Instead, men of good family and social prestige led the fight.

In the light of all the foregoing evidence, how valid is the Woodward thesis? Were race relations, at least in postbellum Virginia, much more amicable and amiable than they became after about the mid-1890's? Did the Negro once ride the trains unsegregated and without resort to discrimination? Was it once possible for him, at least occasionally, to enter restaurants, hotels (especially the dining rooms), waiting rooms, bars, theatres, and other public places of amusement without meeting a wall of segregation and ostracism? And finally, did segregation legislation of the late 1890's and early twentieth century create new mores, instead of merely placing a stamp of legal approval upon those already generally existent?

The Woodward thesis is essentially sound. Of course certain qualifications must be made, but they do not destroy or greatly impair its essential validity. The

Woodward thesis must also be evaluated in the complete context of *The Strange Career of Jim Crow*, where Professor Woodward himself qualifies it, offers it tentatively and with reserve, and denies all claims of a golden age in Southern race relations in the 1870's and 1880's. The danger is that one is tempted to accept the Woodward thesis at complete face value as the whole answer. It is also easy to deduce or conclude too much, as Professor Woodward sometimes does, from relatively few and isolated occurrences.

This much, however, can be said for it in the case of Virginia: While the Negro was increasingly used, abused, and driven from the polls by the politicians in the periods, 1873–1878, and 1884–1902 — the interval being the Readjuster era — at no time was it the general demand of the white populace that the Negro be disfranchised and white supremacy made the law of the land. At the time the railroad segregation statute was passed in 1900, the Negro sat where he pleased and among white passengers on perhaps a majority of the state's railroads. Occasionally the Negro met no segregation when he entered restaurants, bars, waiting rooms, theatres, and other public places of amusement; most of the time, however, he did meet segregation, opposition, or eviction, and this is the weakest part of the Woodward thesis. But it must be remembered that the newspapers and individual authors who commented on the passing scene were essentially conservative and prone to record a Negro's being thrown out of a restaurant, for example, rather than his being served in one. Segregation in these areas does, however, seem to have been more general in Virginia than in two of the most conservative Southern states, South Carolina and Mississippi. Detailed studies have been made of the Negro in these states in this era. There is much in these two works which tends to support the Woodward thesis, thus offsetting some negative findings in the case of Virginia.

The real value of the Woodward thesis is that it furnishes historians with a wholly new and fresh approach to the study of the racial question in the South for the post-Military Reconstruction years. It is a milestone in scholarship which cannot be ignored.

THE DEBATE ON SCHOOL SEGREGATION IN SOUTH CAROLINA, 1868

Delegates to the all-Republican Constitutional Convention of 1868 in South Carolina wanted to make mandatory a minimal exposure to education for all children in the state, and they wanted to endorse the concept that all public schools should be open to all children without regard to race. At the same time, however, they recognized that both white and Negro parents were reluctant to place their children in mixed schools, and they did not want to jeopardize acceptance of the proposed constitution by overriding these sentiments. The result was a report by

From the *Proceedings of the Constitutional Convention of South Carolina Held at Charleston, South Carolina, beginning January 14th and ending March 17th, 1868* (Charleston: Denny & Perry, 1868), pp. 691–94, 702–6.

the Committee on Education which called for compulsory attendance and racially open schools. Still, where it was economically feasible and both Negroes and whites preferred, separate schools could be provided. In areas too poor to afford separation, white and Negro parents retained the option of sending their children to private schools. The following debate suggests the attitudes of the Negro delegates on this subject.

All of the participants are Negroes with the exception of R. G. Holmes, who had been a Boston businessman before coming South after the war; C. P. Leslie, an aging, erratic, and constantly critical New Yorker; and R. J. Donaldson, a transplanted Englishman. Cardozo, chairman of the education committee, had been born in Charleston, educated in the University of Edinburgh, engaged as minister to a congregation in New Haven, Connecticut, and sent to Charleston as an educational missionary immediately after the war. In 1868 he was principal of the leading Negro school in the state. Cain and Wright were Northern Negroes who had come to the State after the war. The remainder were native South Carolinians.

MR. R. C. DeLarge. What does the tenth section of that report say?

Mr. A. C. Richmond. I believe it is the meaning, that if families of white people are not able to send their children to private schools, they shall be obliged to send their children to the public schools, in which all white and colored shall be educated.

Mr. F. L. Cardozo. We only compel parents to send their children to some school, not that they shall send them with the colored children; we simply give those colored children who desire to go to white schools, the privilege to do so.

Mr. A. C. Richmond. By means of moral suasion, I believe nearly all the colored people, as well as a large number of the children of white parents will go to school; such schools as their parents may select. If parents are too proud to take advantage of the means of education afforded, why then I say let their children grow up in ignorance.

Mr. J. A. Chestnut. So far as I have been able to see and judge, this report of the Committee is a sensible one, and ought to be adopted as it stands. How it can affect the rights of the people, or interfere with the spirit of republicanism, I am at a loss to discover. On the contrary, from all the experience I have had among the people, I unhesitatingly declare that no measure adopted by this Convention will be more in consonance with their wishes than this, or more productive of material blessings to all classes. Sir, you cannot by any persuasive and reasonable means establish civilization among an ignorant and degraded community, such as we have in our country. Force is necessary, and, for one, I say let force be used. Republicanism has given us freedom, equal rights, and equal laws. Republicanism must also give us education and wisdom.

It seems that the great difficulty in this section is in the fact that difficulty may arise between the two races in the same school, or that the whites will not send their children to the same schools with the colored children. What of that? Has not this Convention a right to establish a free school system for the benefit of the poorer classes? Undoubtedly. Then if there be a hostile disposition among the whites, an unwillingness to send their children to school, the fault is their own, not ours. Look at the idle youths around us. Is the sight not enough to invigorate every man with a desire to do something to remove this vast weight of ignorance that presses the masses down? I have no desire to curtail the privileges of freemen, but when we look at the opportunities neglected, even by the whites of South Carolina, I must confess that I am more than ever disposed to compel parents, especially of my own race, to send their children to school. If the whites object to it, let it be so. The consequences will rest with themselves.

I hope, therefore, that the motion to strike out the word "compulsory" will be laid upon the table.

Mr. R. H. Cain. It seems to me that we are spending a great deal of unnecessary time in the discussion of this subject. It is true, the question is one of great interest, and there are few who are not anxious that provisions shall be made by this Convention for the education of all classes in the State. But I am confident that it will not be necessary to use compulsion to effect this object. Hence, I am opposed to the insertion of the obnoxious word. I see no necessity for it. You cannot compel parents to send their children to school; and if you could, it would be unwise, impolitic, and injudicious. Massachusetts is fifty years ahead of South Carolina, and, under the circumstances which exist in that State, I might, if a resident, insist upon a compulsory education; but in South Carolina the case is different. There is a class of persons here whose situation, interests and necessities are varied, and controlled by surroundings which do not exist at the North. And justice is demanded for them. To do justice in this matter of education, compulsion is not required. I am willing to trust

the people. They have good sense, and experience itself will be better than all the force you can employ to instill the idea of duty to their children.

Now, as a compromise with the other side, I propose the following amendment, namely that "the General Assembly may require the attendance at either public or private schools," &c.

This is a question that should be left to the Legislature. If the circumstances demand it, compulsion may be used to secure the attendance of pupils; but I do not believe such a contingency ever will occur.

As to the idea that both classes of children will be compelled to go to school together, I do not think it is comprehended in the subject at all. I remember that in my younger days I stumped the State of Iowa for the purpose of having stricken from the Constitution a clause which created distinction of color in the public schools. This was prior to the assembling of the Constitutional Convention. All we claimed was that they should make provision for the education of all the youth. We succeeded, and such a clause was engrafted in the Constitution, and that instrument was ratified by a majority of ten thousand. We said nothing about color. We simply said "youth."

I say to you, therefore, leave this question open. Leave it to the Legislature. I have great faith in humanity. We are in a stage of progress, such as our country never has seen, and while the wheels are rolling on, depend upon it, there are few persons in this country who will not seek to enjoy it by sending their children to school. White or black, all will desire to have their children educated. Let us then make this platform broad enough for all to stand upon without prejudice or objection. The matter will regulate itself, and to the Legislature may safely be confided the task of providing for any emergency which may arise.

Mr. R. G. Holmes. If there is anything we want in this State, it is some measure to compel the attendance of children between the ages of six and sixteen at some school. If it is left to parents, I believe the great majority will lock up their children at home. I hope, therefore, we shall have a law compelling the attendance of all children at school. It is the statute law in Massachusetts, and I hope we will have the provision inserted in our Constitution. The idea that it is not republican to educate children is supremely ridiculous. Republicanism, as has been well said, is not license. No man has the right, as a republican, to put his hand in my pocket, or steal money from it, because he wishes to do it. I can conceive of a way in which my child may be robbed by that system of republicanism which some members have undertaken to defend. My child may be left an orphan, poor and dependent on the kindness of neighbors or friends. They may think it to the best interest of that child to bind it out as an apprentice to some person. My child may be robbed of an education, because the person to whom it was bound does not think it advisable to send that child to school, as there may happen to be some objectionable children in the school. I have seen white children sitting by the side of colored children in school, and observed that there could not have been better friends. I do not want this privilege of attending schools confined to any exclusive class. We want no laws made here to prevent children from attending school. If any one chooses to educate their children in a private school, this law does not debar them that privilege.

* * *

Mr. C. P. Leslie. If our friends from Massachusetts can be kept quiet a little while, it will gratify me exceedingly to have a little talk with them. When this Convention was first called, some of the delegates in the house, and many of the friends outside, if they met with the slightest possible misfortune, if a man lost his watch, or his pocket book, the first thing he did was to run into the menagerie, when some delegate would immediately offer a resolution that some sort of relief should be extended. After a good deal of nonsense, it was at last thought not really proper to present that style of resolution. Time run on, and the few delegates here in this body from somewhere have seemed so to act, that they were picked out, and told by our enemies to do some pretty thing or things, that would, beyond any question, tend to defeat the adoption of the Constitution we are endeavoring to frame for this State, they could not be doing better than they are now. Sometime ago our friends looked anxiously forward to the various questions that should arise. One important question was that of the judiciary. That, fortunately for all, has been settled in a way that gives satisfaction to every reflecting right-minded man in the State. There were a number of questions that directly affected the fate of the pending Constitution. One important question was the homestead, and our friends again looked forward to see what action the delegates would take in that direction. I know the homestead provision put in our Constitution was one of the very best strokes of policy we have yet made. Right upon the heel of that, and at a time when everything is going on sensibly, so that it is believed no power in the State can by any possibility defeat the adoption of our Constitution, comes a proposition that must be odious to a large class of people in the State.

Now, I can live in South Carolina whether the Constitution is adopted or not, and I can vote in this State. I can have every right and privilege that any white voter has; but I say to the colored members of this body if this Constitution is not adopted they cannot do it. I do not suppose, in the present condition of affairs, that we can make a Constitution that is in all respects just exactly what we would have it. There are many good provisions that we may from absolute necessity have to leave out. There are a great many provisions that I myself would be glad to insert in that Constitution, but I will never be guilty of doing an act when my own good sense condemns that act. It is as important to the colored people of the State as to the white; it is important to me, and important to every man in the State, that a fair, liberal, just and generous government should be established. It is important to the rising generation, both white and colored. If you do not happen to get all you want; if you do not want to insert a provision which will endanger the result of the vote on the Constitution when it goes before the people, then for heaven's sake have sense enough to leave it out. Some people think they can come in here and can make just such a Constitution as they in their playful judgment may think proper. They think that a poor miserable South Carolinian can be taken up here and led just where they wish to take him. Another says he shall have nothing but gingerbread; and still another comes from Massachusetts, and insists that this miserable South Carolinian shall eat anything he chooses to cram him with, and brings in a long doctor's bill. Another from Massachusetts says he shall not have anything to drink, and so on until you have enough before you, which, if adopted, will bring our

Constitution beyond any hopes of resurrection.

I appeal to the good sense of the delegates, to reflect that every time you undertake to force a people to do what you know they do not want to do, it can never be carried out. I am to-day a South Carolinian; I am going to live and die a loyal man; to be loyal to the government, but by the eternal heavens I will never be forced to do what in my own judgment no one has the right to force upon me. Who is going to execute this law if made? That is a direct question, and I want the delegates from Massachusetts to come up squarely and fairly and answer it. Our friend from Massachusetts undertakes to tell us the loyal men are going to do it. Who are they? Are they the black people in the State? You cannot force them any more than you can the whites. There is no use making a law unless you can enforce it; but if you undertake to go on with this wild business, I warn you of the consequences.

Mr. F. L. Cardozo. The gentleman from Barnwell (*Mr. Leslie*) has made an appeal to the fear of the colored delegates on this floor, by holding up before them the bugbear of the defeat of our Constitution. I would simply say, that I do not think there is a colored delegate but what knows that we have carried the Convention against the white people of this State, and will carry the Constitution also. I will qualify my language, by saying that we do not fear those whom the gentleman from Barnwell tells us to fear.

Mr. R. J. Donaldson. Will the gentleman be kind enough to inform the Convention how many native born South Carolinians are upon the Committee on Education?

Mr. F. L. Cardozo. There is but one Massachusetts man on the Committee.

Mr. C. P. Leslie. Did any South Carolinian vote for that provision? If so, I would like to know it?

Mr. F. L. Cardozo. I would say that one style of argument, of appealing to our fears, or cowardice, or our unmanliness, is scarcely worth noticing.

Mr. C. P. Leslie. The gentleman has asserted or misstated what I said. I did not appeal to the cowardice of the colored delegates; I appealed simply to their good sense.

Mr. F. L. Cardozo. I still maintain my position, that the style of argument to which I have alluded is low, mean, and unmanly. I desire, in the first place, to divest this question of the false issues which some cunning political demagogues on the floor have connected with it. They have said this section would compel colored and white children to go together in the schools.

Mr. J. J. Wright. I rise to a point of order. I object to the words "political demagogues," used by the gentleman in his argument.

Mr. C. P. Leslie. He had reference to himself; what you do want to interrupt him for?

Mr. F. L. Cardozo. I referred to the gentleman from Barnwell.

Mr. C. P. Leslie. I refer to him.

Mr. F. L. Cardozo. I will state again, that it is the habit of some members of the Convention, when they want to defeat a measure, to connect false issues with it, and make it appear as odious as possible. I ask members to look at the strategy kept up by members of the opposition. They have said that we compel white and colored to go together in these schools, and by that means they attempt to defeat this section. Their assertion is ungentlemanly, and it is untrue.

The hour of six having arrived, the President announced the Convention adjourned.

The Convention assembled at 10 A. M., and was called to order by the President.

Prayer was offered by the Rev. B. F. Jackson.

The roll was called, and a quorum answering to their names, the President announced the Convention ready to proceed to business.

The Journal of yesterday was read and confirmed.

The Convention resumed the consideration of the fourth section of the report of the Committee on the Executive part of the Constitution, providing that it shall be the duty of the General Assembly to provide for the compulsory attendance, at either public or private schools, of all children between the ages of six and sixteen years, not physically or mentally disabled, for a term equivalent to at least twenty-four months.

The first question was striking out the word "compulsory."

Mr. F. L. Cardozo. Before I resume my remarks this morning, I would ask the favor of the Convention, and especially the opposition, to give me their close attention, and I think I can settle this matter perfectly satisfactory to every one in the house.

It was argued by some yesterday, with some considerable weight, that we should do everything in our power to incorporate into the Constitution all possible measures that will conciliate those opposed to us.

No one would go farther in conciliating others than I would. But those whom we desire to conciliate consist of three different classes, and we should be careful, therefore, what we do to conciliate.

In the first place there is an element which is opposed to us, no matter what we do will never be conciliated. It is not that they are opposed so much to the Constitution we may frame, but they are opposed to us sitting in Convention. Their objection is of such a fundamental and radical nature, that any attempt to frame a Constitution to please them would be utterly abortive.

In the next place, there are those who are doubtful, and gentlemen here say if we frame a Constitution to suit these parties they will come over with us. They are only waiting, and I will say these parties do not particularly care what kind of a Constitution you frame, they only want to see whether it is going to be successful, and if it is, they will come any way.

Then there is a third class who honestly question our capacity to frame a Constitution. I respect that class, and believe if we do justice to them, laying our corner-stone on the sure foundation of republican government and liberal principles, the intelligence of that class will be conciliated, and they are worthy of conciliation.

Before I proceed to discuss the question, I want to divest it of all false issues, of the imaginary consequences that some

gentlemen have illogically thought will result from the adoption of this section with the word compulsory. They affirm that it compels the attendance of both white and colored children in the same schools. There is nothing of the kind in the section. It means nothing of the kind, and no such construction can be legitimately placed upon it. It simply says all the children shall be educated; but how is left with the parents to decide. It is left to the parent to say whether the child shall be sent to a public or private school. The eleventh section has been referred to as bearing upon this section. I will ask attention to this fact. The eleventh section does not say, nor does the report in any part say there shall not be separate schools. There can be separate schools for white and colored. It is simply left so that if any colored child wishes to go to a white school, it shall have the privilege to do so. I have no doubt, in most localities, colored people would prefer separate schools, particularly until some of the present prejudice against their race is removed.

Hinton Rowan Helper: THE NEGROES IN NEGROLAND

THERE ARE now in the United States of America thirty millions of white people, who are (or ought to be) bound together by the ties of a kindred origin, by the affinities of a sameness of noble purpose, by the links of a common nationality, and by the cords of an inseparable destiny. We have here also, unfortunately for us all, four millions of black people, whose ancestors, like themselves, were never known (except in very rare

instances, which form the exceptions to a general rule) to aspire to any other condition than that of base and beastlike slavery. These black people are, by nature, of an exceedingly low and grovelling disposition. They have no trait of character that is lovely or admirable. They are not high-minded, enterprising, nor prudent. In no age, in no part of the world, have they, of themselves, ever projected or advanced any public or pri-

From Hinton Rowan Helper, *The Negroes in Negroland; the Negro in America; and Negroes Generally* (New York: G. W. Carleton, 1868), pp. viii–x, xii–xiv.

vate interest, nor given expression to any thought or sentiment that could worthily elicit the praise, or even the favorable mention, of the better portion of mankind. Seeing, then, that the negro does, indeed, belong to a lower and inferior order of beings, why, in the name of Heaven, why should we forever degrade and disgrace both ourselves and our posterity by entering, of our own volition, into more intimate relations with him? May God, in his restraining mercy, forbid that we should ever do this most foul and wicked thing!

Acting under the influence of that vile spirit of deception and chicanery which is always familiar with every false pretence, the members of a Radical Congress, the editors of a venal press, and other peddlers of perverted knowledge, are now loudly proclaiming that nowhere in our country, henceforth, must there be any distinction, any discrimination, on account of color; thereby covertly inculcating the gross error of inferring or supposing that color is the only difference — and that a very trivial difference — between the whites and the blacks! Now, once and for all, in conscientious deference to truth, let it be distinctly made known and acknowledged, that, in addition to the black and baneful color of the negro, there are numerous other defects, physical, mental, and moral, which clearly mark him, when compared with the white man, as a very different and inferior creature. While, therefore, with an involuntary repugnance which we cannot control, and with a wholesome antipathy which it would be both unnatural and unavailing in us to attempt to destroy, we behold the crime-stained blackness of the negro, let us, also, at the same time, take cognizance of

His low and compressed Forehead;

His hard, thick Skull;

His small, backward-thrown Brain;

His short, crisp Hair;

His flat Nose;

His thick Lips;

His projecting, snout-like Mouth;

His strange, Eunuch-toned Voice;

The scantiness of Beard on his Face;

The Toughness and Unsensitiveness of his Skin;

The Thinness and Shrunkenness of his Thighs;

His curved Knees;

His calfless Legs;

His low, short Ankles;

His long, flat Heels;

His glut-shaped Feet;

The general Angularity and Oddity of his Frame;

The Malodorous Exhalations from his Person;

His Puerility of Mind;

His Inertia and Sleepy-headedness;

His proverbial Dishonesty;

His predisposition to fabricate Falsehoods; and

His Apathetic Indifference to all Propositions and Enterprises of Solid Merit.

Many other differences might be mentioned; but the score and more of obvious and undeniable ones here enumerated ought to suffice for the utter confusion and shame of all those disingenuous politicians and others, who, knowing better, and who are thus guilty of the crime of defeating the legitimate ends of their own knowledge, would, for mere selfish and partisan purposes, convey the delusive impression that there is no other difference than that of color.

❀   ❀   ❀

There are many points of general dissatisfaction and dispute, which should not, on any account, be overlooked in the discussion of the subjects here presented. One of these is, that white people, whose reason and honor have not been vitiated, object to close relationship with negroes, not wishing to live with them in the same house; not wishing to fellowship with them in the same society, assembly, or congregation; not wishing to ride with them in the same omnibus, car, or carriage; and not wishing to mess with them at the same table, whether at a hotel, in a restaurant, on a steamer, or elsewhere. Now, any and every white person who does not think and act in strict accordance with the just and pure promptings here indicated, is, in reality, a most unworthy and despicable representative of his race. Even the lower animals, the creatures of mere instinct — the beasts, the birds, and the fishes — many distinct species of which are apparently quite similar, set us daily and hourly examples of the eminent propriety of each kind forming and maintaining separate communities of their own; and so we always find them — in herds, in flocks, and in shoals. How can the negro be a fit person to occupy, in any capacity, our houses or our hotels, our theatres or our churches, our schools or our colleges, our steamers or our vehicles, or any other place or places of uncommon comfort and convenience, which owe their creation, their proper uses, and their perpetuity, to the whites alone — places and improvements about which the negro, of himself, is, and always has been, absolutely ignorant and indifferent? Neither in his own country nor elsewhere has the negro ever built a house or a theatre; he has never erected a church nor a college; he has never constructed a steamer nor a railroad, nor a railroad-car — nor, except when under the special direction and control of superior intelligence, has he ever invented or manufactured even the minutest ap-

pendage of any one of the distinctive elements or realities of human progress. Yet, let this not, by any means, be understood as an argument, nor even as a hint, in behalf of slavery. It is to the great and lasting honor of the Republic that slavery in the United States is abolished forever. In losing her slaves, the South lost nothing that was worth the keeping. Had slavery only been abolished by law many years ago, our whole country would be infinitely better off to-day.

Never will it be possible for the compiler to erase from his memory the feelings of weighty sadness and disgust which overcame him, a few months since, when, while sojourning in the city of Washington, he walked, one day, into the Capitol, and, leisurely passing into the galleries of the two houses of Congress, beheld there, uncouthly lounging and dozing upon the seats, a horde of vile, ignorant, and foul-scented negroes. He was perplexed, shocked, humiliated, and indignant — and could not sit down. With merited emotions of bitterness and contempt for those narrow-minded white men, through whose detestable folly and selfishness so great an outrage against public propriety and decency had been perpetrated, he turned away — indeed, it was not in his power to contemplate with calmness that motley and monstrous manifestation of national incongruity, ugliness, and disgrace. Then it was that, for the first time in his life, he wished himself a Hercules, in order that he might be able to clean, thoroughly and at once, those Augean stables of the black ordure and Radical filth which, therein and elsewhere, had already accumulated to an almost insufferable excess. It was the powerful and long-lingering momentum of the impressions received on that occasion, more than any other circumstance, that gave definite form and resolution to the purpose (although the idea had been previously entertained) of preparing this compilation. The object of the compiler will have been well attained if the work aids materially in more fully convincing his countrymen, North, South, East and West, that negro equality, negro supremacy, and negro domination, as now tyrannically enforced at the point of the bayonet, are cruel and atrocious innovations, which ought to be speedily terminated.

Dr. James R. Sparkman: THE NEGRO

THE NEGRO is the all absorbing topic of the day. In State & Church he is the all engrossing subject of attention, solicitude and study. Having been made a political integer in the government, which enfranchised him, with all the rights & privileges of citizenship without consideration, or preparation for the very responsible duties involved, and having in the same day occupied the dual position of Slave & Freedman — we propose to consider his *past*, as slave — & his *present*, as Freedman — with the view of determining his future as citizen.

This can only be satisfactorily done by one whose experience with the race has resulted from constant intercourse & direct contact with them as a people under both antebellum to postbellum regimes. My authority to speak is derived from the fact that I was born among slaves, raised with them, was a slave holder by inheritance, and have had for more than half a century daily observation & experience in studying & noting their habits, character and race proclivities. I will not pause to consider the endearments & childhood with nurse, old mama, & foster mother, nor will I dwell upon the happy days of my boyhood with playmate, selected from a most exemplary colored family by adopted parents (who had no children) & assigned to me exclusively as playmate, companion & body servant, with mutual attachments we were inseparable, and whenever my partiality for him excited the jealousy or envy of others, he was ready to justify & excuse it with the remark, that "we belonged to each other till death" — Premising this much, I date my opportunity for mature practical observation & experience from the date of my medical diploma — April 1836 —

Immediately after graduation, I located for practice on the Pee Dee River, in the County of Georgetown — in one of the most densely populated sections of Rice culture. In less than two years I became the regular medical attendant & advisor on upwards of thirty plantations, or rice Estates, with an aggregate population of about 4000 Slaves. In addition I had the families of several hundred whites as *owners*, & *overseers*, with all of whom I held friendly & confidential association, thus enabling me whilst studying the idiosyncrasies & normal condition of the

From a manuscript in the Sparkman Family Papers, Southern Historical Collection, University of North Carolina, Chapel Hill, N. C. While this manuscript was undated and unsigned, internal analysis indicates that it was written in 1889 and the handwriting suggests that the author was Dr. James R. Sparkman. Possibly, Dr. Sparkman read the paper at a meeting of a local agricultural society. The editor is grateful to (Mrs.) Hattie Sparkman Witte of Columbia, South Carolina, for her generous assent to the publication of this essay.

slaves as field laborers, also to note their habits & character as domestics in family or household service. This latter class were conspicuous for their politeness, civility, & gentility, being directly under the exemplary & refining influence of the highest type of Civilization in the Country — the Educated Southern Slaveholders.

This field I occupied uninterruptedly until the day of Emancipation, all through the War. My intercourse with the sick & well was constant; responding day & night to all professional calls & when necessary, spending entire nights in the sick chambers of these slaves, directly on the banks of the ricefields, at all seasons of the year, in the thickest fights with disease and miasmatic pestilence. Since 1865 when Freedom was proclaimed & accepted, I have occupied the same location, but with a more limited field from the changes of population & disturbance in social relations and agricultural matters.

But with the insight and cumulative experience of over fifty consecutive years, I think it will hardly be denied that I have had exceptional opportunities for knowing & understanding the habits & attributes of the colored man, both as slave & freedman.

Early in practice I met with a few slaves imported direct from Africa & knew many of their immediate descendants & families. They were generally of small stature, but physically strong & able, good workers, and of normal longevity. I found one of these men in my gang when I reached my majority & took possession of my small inheritance. He had for many years filled the responsible post of "barnyard watchman." His fidelity was conspicuous & commended him to special consideration. During his last illness, I was studious to administer to his every want and comfort, and, finding him sinking, I asked specially what he wanted to eat. To my great horror he replied, "nice fat baby, Massa. I want to suck the sweet bones of fat baby hand — too nice." Then in the very hour of dissolution (about 80 years of age) this man's cannibal appetite asserted itself altho so long removed from all savage indulgencies. What a commentary!

As a slave the negro was generally docile, tractable and readily trained to duties & habits of trust & responsibility. It was a trite saying with him that "good massa make good nigger & bad massa make bad nigger." But all slaveholders were assumed to be cruel taskmasters by outsiders who knew practically nothing of the institution of slavery. Our federal foes were not prepared, therefore, to find with rare exceptions, the slaves of the entire South faithful & industrious to the very end of the military struggle all around them during four long years of hostilities. Under Slavery the relation between the whites & blacks was paternal & confiding; so that a master blessed with offspring to inherit his Estate was always considered by the slaves a source of comfort & satisfaction, for they held in dread the possibility of being left "Estate niggers," viz without hereditary ownership. History can not deprive the black man *as a slave* of his highest claim to exemplary fidelity & good character, during the strong temptations & many opportunities for combined effort & insurrectionary plots for personal freedom all through the interstate war; & I bear most willing testimony, personally, to his loyalty & fidelity to the helpless families & defenseless children, entrusted to his care during the four years struggle which was to decide his own future. So much for the civilising tendency & restraining influence of slavery. Removed from this paternal guidance & control of the white master the second volume of his history opens, & will unfold & determine the danger of his relapse into the savage proclivities of his race, & returning to his idols.

Constitutionally the negro is Emotional, in no case more pronounced than in his religion. Race tendencies are hard to overcome & obliterate. For a season civilised teachers and religious training may apparently bear encouraging fruit, but like the cannibal appetite, idolatrous voodooism may unexpectedly rise to the surface & disappoint. An apt illustration is furnished in the lamentable experience of that sainted good man, the Rev. Alexander Glennie of All Saints Waccamaw. Far more than thirty years of his life have been devoted to missionary work in a parish with about Six thousand Slaves — scattered along on adjoining large rice Estates, a distance of near thirty miles, with the central church & two other Chapels located for the convenience of the whites. Each plantation had its separate chapel or building for religious teaching & training of the Slaves. The Rector of the Parish was assisted by one or more archivists, so that church services were held almost every day or night in the year, in one or other of these chapels. Mr. Glennie was for more than thirty years teaching, preaching, baptising, & receiving into Holy Communion this large flock & was esteemed one of the most successful & exemplary missionary pioneers of our Church in the whole South. But alas he lived to see (as he expressed it) the labors of his life time dissipated & lost in a single day. In one or more of his cherished congregations they flatly refused his ministrations & declined the further services of the church as soon as their freedom was acknowledged & accepted by the whites. But more than this, on one plantation, where more than ordinary attention had

been given to their religious training, there was an open relapse into Feticism [Fetishism] or *Voodooism* which was brought to the special attention of the late Bishop Davis, who with the Rev. Mr. Glennie visited this plantation. After returning from their visit the Bishop told me that for the first time in his life he had been brought in personal contact with the devil & that he was powerless. Military interference was afterwards invoked before the outbreak could be controlled. This case is cited simply to illustrate how short the step from civilisation back to heathenism, with *race tendencies* prompting under almost the first breath of absolute unrestrained freedom.

We now come to the general results of Emancipation as developed in the quarter of a Century since accepted Freedom. Has the negro retrograded, or advanced; & if any, what [are] the evidences of his material prosperity to day? We will analyse him morally, intellectually, physically & industrially. Our purpose will be more readily conceived by noting (& remembering) some of the acknowledged constitutional defects & attributes of the *African race*. They are easily grouped — notoriously dishonest, untruthful, unchaste, indolent, idle, selfish, vicious, treacherous & unreliable.

Born a *thief,* the twin vice *lying* necessarily follows & hand in hand they go together. Without chastity his bestial appetites and animal passions early developed, are constantly tempting and leading to criminal indulgences. He is aggressive but cowardly & sullen in his treachery. Remember these *race* proclivities, whilst comparing their present *post*bellum condition with their former *ante*bellum surroundings. Freedom found them semi-civilised & semi-Christianised in comfortable houses & homes, well fed, well clothed, well cared for in sickness & old age, & their physical condition carefully developed by the selection of work suited to their capacity. Under new relations, as laborers, they were invited to remain where they were, without the expense of building or renting houses & lands; to cultivate the plantations & to share liberally the rewards of their industry; all taxes & machinery for agricultural progress being provided & advances of provisions & necessary comforts arranged by the land owners or proprietors. The theory was plausible & their prosperity and independence seemed well nigh assured. But unfortunately for the newly fledged freedman, he had adopted the idea that the Government was also to furnish him land & the mule to work it. His own manual exertions were, consequently, very reluctantly given, or withheld altogether, and at the end of the year he was dissatisfied with results. Then began his assertion of freedom by the violation of contracts & obligations; neglecting his own crops & working out to the detriment of his Employer, & finally moving & migrating from place to place, seeking such changes as would relieve him from personal supervision & restraint. Many abandoned their plantation accommodations, and settled in adjacent pine lands & swamps, stealing & carrying off all accessible material for building rude huts wherever they could purchase an acre or two of land, secured from all personal liability or pecuniary obligation by the "homestead act" of which they soon learned to avail themselves. Even these interruptions to prosperity would have been overcome if the Southern negroes had been left to regulate & equalise matters with the Southern whites in accord with their mutual interests. But political emergencies demanded him as a link in the party chain by which the States in their plurality work together as a government unit. Political equality had been inaugurated & this begat the

ambition for social equality and altho the political rulers & wise men of the dominant party of today may easily review & discover their mistakes in legislating for the negro without qualification, education or preparation for self government, the poor South has to endure [the] vexatious evils resulting therefrom. But let me go back to our immediate subject, the *present condition of the freedmen* as to material prosperity. I can most truly bear witness that they are not as comfortably housed, as well fed, clothed, or provided for in sickness & the infirmities of age as formerly. I have not seen an all wool blanket among them in ten years. Their clothing is mostly of thin cheap material, especially the women and children. All hygienic considerations being entirely overlooked, such as cleanliness, good drinking water, drainage around their settlements and well cooked food, with comfortable sleeping apartments. During the first decade of freedom their numbers were largely decimated by invasion of contagious diseases. Within the last decade they have notably suffered from lung diseases with increased mortality — Consumption heading the list. As to fertility, the rate of birth may be normal, but fewer children are raised & I do not think that the increase of population is as large as many suppose. I mean in the seaboard Counties. The next Census will determine the aggregate of the State. There is only occasionally local suffering calling for neighborhood relief. Pauperism is provided for by the County, but it requires constant vigilance to protect against the abuse of this Charity. There is a thriftless class scattered all through the woodlands, remote from the public highways & sheltered from general observation, who manage to live, that is, do not die of starvation, but a glance at their dens assured you that they do not make an *honest* living. The whole colored race use tobacco freely, & are fond of intoxicating drinks, but I do not think that they indulge to greater excess than the whites.

As to their intellectual advancement, it can not be denied that for many years the expenditure for Free Schools gave no satisfactory returns. Ignorant inexperienced teachers made no progress with their more ignorant but less pretentious pupils. Latterly the prospect is more hopeful, but still discouraging in all the *rural* districts. The opening of free schools for two or three months in the year has proven inadequate for mental progress. The little gained in one session is lost before the return of another school term. But the parents are willing & anxious that their children should learn, & in many instances the free schools with colored teachers have been deserted for smaller private schools with white teachers. The School Commiss'r (under a political compromise) is a color'd man. To the *party* man, the spoils of office are here, as elsewhere, attractive & irresistible.

As to *marriage,* I fear that few regard it as sacred & holy. Voluntary separation, or desertion, leaving offspring to the care & support of the mother is of constant occurrence; & infidelity generally is *without loss of caste or character.* I have in memory at this moment a much respected color'd man, who for many years served satisfactorily as Sexton of Church, of which he was a member & communed regularly, & was exemplary in most of his ways; but his master, a clergyman, told me that altho' he never knew him to be dishonest, or untruthful, still he lacked the one cardinal virtue, *chastity,* for he had two wives with separate families. The Church is attractive to most negroes. Almost every adult belongs to some one of the different denominations who strive against each other for memberships.

Their contributions are liberal, but in this matter their clergy & leaders are exacting & grinding. My observations lead me to believe that the church is regarded by many of its members more as a *social but secret society,* from which all mandates and decrees emanating, are to be regarded more authoritative & binding than the laws of the commonwealth or, as they express it, the laws of the white man. I have good reason to know that their preachers are the exponents or mouth pieces of their political tactics, or party combinations & secret resolves as to party action. Also that one of their fundamental teachings is not to bear witness, or go against their color. There is an inherent distrust and hatred of the white race, which over rides all moral obligations, & with extreme reluctance I testify my belief, that the violation of the most sacred oath is condoned by their religious leaders, as well as by the race at large. The presence of a white Christian brother is never invited, & would doubtless be considered obtrusive at their local prayer meetings. Their whole religious worship is proverbially emotional, frequently running into boisterous shoutings, with noisy demonstrations of hands & feet, and extravagant, wild, hysterical gyrations of the body, which are contagious & Exhaustive; sometimes ending in a swoon or semicataleptic condition. Especially emotional [are] their funeral gatherings, and when conducted by torchlight the whole ceremony seems to be a mimicry of the savage war dance. I would not intentionally do injustice to their better class of pulpit men or regularly appointed clergy by including them all under one classification of color, for I know many of them to be discreet, moderate, good men; but I allude chiefly to that class of licentiates, or plantation "locals" by whom the masses are to be leavened. Most of these are influential, leading, but ignorant presuming men, who obtain or accept & use their appointments as a cloak for lust & libertinism. The *average* "class leader" of the rice field plantations, and the small country congregation in rural districts without regular meeting houses or church edifices, is proverbially corrupt and unworthy. As disseminators of immorality in their flocks they notoriously abuse their high calling.

Thus far I have been considering the *race* or mass of color'd citisens travelling from a semi Christianised start on their journey to the goal of material prosperity, on which "Freedom" is expected to prepare & fit them for good citisenship. We will now consider their claims to *industry*, & especially in this portion of the black district, so called. In this County alone there are upwards of 46000 Acres of cleared cultivable tide lands suited to the growth of rice, one of the most productive crops of the South, and most easily marketed. In addition there are 10,000 acres of provision lands adjoining, of uplands formerly cultivated for the maintenance & support of our antebellum population. Rice has always been the specialty of culture in this County, & there was ample force of laborers to cultivate our whole available territory (56,000 acres). But since 1865 the area of Rice Culture in Georgetown Co. has not averaged more than 15000 acres, the present yield per acre scarcely reaching an average of 24 Bushels against 40 to 45 bushels before freedom. This results from unsatisfactory preparation of the soil & imperfect cultivation, with slovenly, wasteful harvesting. Very many have withdrawn from the rice fields. The younger bucks, as soon as they get beyond parental control, abandon field labor & seek a precarious living at job work, migrate to the towns & villages, or engage in [the] demoralising nomadic life

of Turpentine farming. The women for field work generally classify themselves as *half hands* & their children as a rule are not taught to work *regularly*. Hence the effective labor of every plantation is diminished, and practically there is a deficiency. Again there is increasing reluctance to perform manual labor, either for their own comfort, or the interest of the Employer. Dilapidated buildings, decayed fencing, uncultivated uplands & abandoned rice fields, from one river to another all through the rice region proclaim in a single word the condition of proprietor & Employee — "unthrifty" — viz. barely living, no material improvement or prosperity. This will not be denied by any one familiar with the resources of the planters, & the commercial transactions of the County in Agricultural products.

In morals they have also retrograded. Petty larcenies are more common, stealing from each other as often as from the whites. But the damning blot of character, under which they stand openly impeached, is the large & increasing number of cases of that nameless, unmentionable atrocity, calling throughout the entire South for the most summary proceeding under the lawless Lynch. Mythologically speaking, so long as *Venus* is the Evening Star of the Negro, *Jupiter* & *Mars* must and will prove the guiding planets of the Caucasian — nothing more need be said.[1]

A word about the Mulattoes. They are considered more brainy, & generally more intelligent than the blacks. Certain it is that they exercise more influence over the masses, & thereby monopolise most

---

[1] The atrocity to which the author refers is rape. He means to suggest that whenever the brilliant beauty of the white woman (symbolized by Venus) attracts the Negro, fathers and husbands (symbolized by Jupiter and Mars) must stand ready to defend her in a warlike manner.

of the higher appointments to public office. They are more ambitious of distinction, & claim superiority as representatives of the color'd race, which is generally accorded them. The foremost political agitators & office seekers are of mixed blood. Their platform is universal equality in all the avenues of life. Socially, politically, in church & State, *Equality* is the banner under which they march, as proclaimed by their press, from their Pulpit & in the forum. Their claims are based upon their numerical strength as an integral element of the Federal unit by which the States are Constitutionally bound together as a Republican Representative Government. Forgetful of the Constitutional provisions reserved by each State to control within its limits the Election franchise, they are blindly looking to the Republican Party of the North for such legislation as will give them *race* Equality at the South, albeit *practically* it is denied them among hypocritical, so called, best friends, throughout the whole country.

A few negrophilists and itinerant lecturers & hirelings would have us believe that no race of people in history have ever made such rapid progress in civilisation & advancement in the science of government as the negro since his Emancipation from Slavery 25 years ago. The problem of man's capacity for self government, with the whites, is still *sub judice;* its first demonstration will hardly come from any half civilised blacks. Endowed schools, academies, & universities are paraded in view as illustrations of progressive educational facilities. Doubtless they will bear legitimate fruit, & I would say encourage and *multiply* them; & God speed the good work of providing capable, successful *teachers* for the masses in our midst of a semiheathen race who are clamorous for social equality, & Christian brotherhood before they have made any worthy advances in morality, in accepted religion, in intellectual culture, or industrial habits to justify their promotion to unqualified citisenship. Vice & ignorance must be controlled before the negro millennium is reached. Education alone can save the South from black domination & miscegenation, or the alternatives, revolution, expatriation, or extermination. Political sycophants are abroad & have polluted the streams of life! We are in dangerous straits.

George Washington Cable: THE SILENT SOUTH

Unlike Helper in that he speaks for the upper echelon in Southern society, and unlike his fellow patrician Sparkman in that he speaks for rather than against the Negro, George Washington Cable was clearly the Southern white who did most to promote the cause of civil rights for Negroes in the decades following the Civil War. Son of a New Orleans slaveholding family, wounded in the Confederate service, and a rising literary eminence, Cable had, he felt, every right to command attention from his peers. In New Orleans during Reconstruction he had objected vigorously against the separation of Negro children in the public schools. But he did not prolong his protest. Instead he channeled his

From "The Silent South," *The Century Magazine,* XXX (September, 1885), 674–691.

reforming energies into a rewarding attack on the prison and convict-lease systems in the South. Even the virtual nullification of the Civil Rights acts by the Supreme Court in 1883 did not greatly excite him. Cable was brought back to the issue of Negro rights, he testified later, by an incident he observed on a train bound for Louisville. A well-dressed, obviously cultured Negro woman and her daughter had been pressed in upon a coach already overcrowded with nineteen convicts, filthy and in chains. This discomfort and indignity had been forced upon her while the white coach rode nearly empty. The result, delayed by months of careful research and writing, appeared in The Century Magazine *in January, 1885, as "The Freedman's Case in Equity." This article was both an indictment of the South's treatment of the Negro (presented only in the most general terms because Cable did not want to lose the ear of the opposition), and a plea to the sense of justice among upper-class Southerners for "public equality" for the Negro.*

Mild as Cable's statement had been, it was met by a flood of vituperation. He was a traitor, a mercenary writer exploiting Southern misery, an advocate of racial ruin and social violence. "You can form no idea of how bitter the feeling is against you," reported one friend, "as bitter as it used to be against Garrison & men of his way of thinking in ante-bellum times."* Cable underwent eight months of the most vitriolic abuse and then in September, 1885, he published his reply, "The Silent South." Considering himself freed from his previous restraint by the excesses of his opponents, he now catalogued a distressing array of injustices inflicted upon Negroes in public places. Working carefully, he attempted to explain this discrimination as the result of a confusion between civil rights and social rights, and to allay white fear that yielding to the Negro his civil rights would lead to social equality and racial amalgamation. The way out, as Cable seemed to see it, was through a pattern of cultural pluralism which was even then evolving. When thinking whites realized the justice and practical sense of removing restrictions upon the Negro's civil rights and did so, Negroes of high capacities would be elevated in their own societies. That elevation would be signalized by genteel behavior and an ability to use to advantage the best public facilities — the theater, the opera, first-class accommodations on common carriers — along with the better class of whites. But all of this did not mean social equality, for that was a matter of personal taste and choice, as much on the Negro side as on the white. History and common sense observation showed that the races had remained and would remain apart in all social relations, and refrain from that ultimate in integration, miscegenation, because each race was ruled by "the better dictates of reason and the ordinary natural preferences of like for like." In the Cable system black would thus be separated but black would not be bad.

* Quoted in Arlin Turner, *George W. Cable: A Biography* (Baton Rouge: The Louisiana State University Press, 1966), p. 198. The material used in this headnote has been ruled by Professor Turner's study.

BUT NOW that we have clearly made out exactly *what* this immovable hostility is, the question follows — and half the nation are asking it to-day with perplexed brows — *why* is it? Yet the answer is simple. Many white people of the South sincerely believe that the recognition of rights proposed in the old Civil Rights bills or in "The Freedman's Case in Equity" *would precipitate a social chaos.* They believe Civil Rights means Social Equality. This may seem a transparent error, but certainly any community in the world that believed it, would hold the two ideas in equal abomination; and it is because of the total unconsciousness and intense activity of this error at the South, and the subtle sense of unsafety that naturally accompanies it — it is because of this, rather than for any lack of clearness in its statement of the subject, that the article on "The Freedman's Case in Equity" is so grossly misinterpreted even by some who undoubtedly wish to be fair. That this is the true cause of the misinterpretation is clear in the fact that from the first printing of the article until now the misconstruction has occurred only among those whose thinking still runs in the grooves of the old traditions.

Nothing in that paper touches or seeks to touch the domain of social privileges. The standing of the magazine in which it appears is guarantee against the possibility of the paper containing any such insult to the intelligence of enlightened society. Social equality is a fool's dream. The present writer wants quite as little of it as the most fervent traditionist of the most fervent South. The North, the West, the East, and the rest of the intelligent world, want quite as little of it as the South wants. Social equality can never exist where a community, numerous enough to assert itself, is actuated, as every civilized community is, by an intellectual and moral ambition. No form of laws, no definition of rights, from Anarchy to Utopia, can bring it about. The fear that this or that change will produce it ought never to be any but a fool's fear. And yet there is this to be added; that no other people in America are doing so much *for* Social equality as those who, while they warmly charge it upon others, are themselves thrusting arbitrary and cheap artificial distinctions into the delicate machinery of society's self-distribution as it revolves by the power of our natural impulses, and of morality, personal interest, and personal preferences. This, of course, is not the intention, and even these persons retard only incidentally, unawares and within narrow limits, nature's social distributions, while taking diligent and absolutely needless pains to hold apart two races which really have no social affinity at all.

Do we charge any bad intention or conscious false pretense? Not at all! They are merely making the double mistake of first classing as personal social privileges certain common impersonal rights of man, and then turning about and treating them as rights definable by law — which social amenities are not and cannot be.

For the sake of any who might still misunderstand, let us enlarge here a moment. The family relation has *rights.* Hence marital laws and laws of succession. But beyond the family circle there are no such things as social *rights;* and when our traditionalists talk about a too hasty sympathy having "fixed by enactment" the negro's *social* and civil rights they talk — unwisely. All the relations of life that go by *impersonal right* are Civil relations. All that go by *personal choice* are Social relations. The one is all of right, it makes no difference who we are;

the other is all of choice, and it makes all the difference who we are; and it is no little fault against ourselves as well as others, to make confusion between the two relations. For the one we make laws; for the other every one consults his own pleasure; and the law that refuses to protect a civil right, construing it a social privilege, deserves no more regard than if it should declare some social privilege to be a civil right. Social *choice,* civil *rights;* but a civil *privilege,* in America, is simply heresy against both our great national political parties at once. Now, "The Freedman's Case in Equity" pleads for not one thing belonging to the domain of social relations. Much less the family relation; it does not hint the faintest approval of any sort of admixture of the two bloods. Surely nothing that a man can buy a ticket for anonymously at a ticket-seller's hand-hole confers the faintest right to even a bow of recognition that any one may choose to withhold. But what says the other side? "The South will never adopt the suggestion of the *social intermingling* of the two races." So they beg the question of equity, and suppress a question of civil right by simply mis-calling it "social intermingling"; thus claiming for it that sacredness from even the law's control which only social relations have, and the next instant asserting the determination of one race to "control the social relations," so-called, of two. Did ever champions of a cause with blanker simplicity walk into a sack and sew up its mouth? Not only thus, but from within it they announce a doctrine that neither political party in our country would venture to maintain; for no party dare say that in these United States there is any room for any one class of citizens to fasten arbitrarily upon any other class of citizens a *civil status* from which no merit of intelligence, virtue, or

possessions can earn an extrication. We have a country large enough for all the *unsociality* anybody may want, but not for *incivility* either by or without the warrant of law. . . .

"Neither race wants it," says one; alluding to that common, undivided participation in the enjoyment of civil rights, for which the darker race has been lifting one long prayer these twenty years, and which he absurdly miscalls "social intermingling." "The interest, as the inclination, of both races is against it," he adds. "Here the issue is made up."

But he mistakes. The issue is not made up here at all. It is not a question of what the *race* wants, but of *what the individual wants and has a right to.* Is that question met? No. Not a line has been written to disprove the individual freedman's title to these rights; but pages, to declare that his race does not want them and shall not have them if it does. Mark the contradiction. It does not want them — it shall not have them! Argument unworthy of the nursery; yet the final essence of all the other side's arguments. They say the colored race wants a participation in public rights separate from the whites; and that anyhow it has got to take that or nothing; "The white and black races in the South *must* walk apart." One writer justifies this on the belief of a natal race instinct; but says that if there were no such thing the South "would, by every means in its power, so strengthen the race *prejudice* that it would do the work and hold the stubbornness and strength of instinct." Could any one more distinctly or unconsciously waive the whole question of right and wrong? Yet this is the standpoint on which it is proposed to meet the freedmen's case *in equity.* Under the heat of such utterances how the substance melts out of their writer's later proposition for the South to solve the question "without passion or prejudice and with full regard for the unspeakable equities it holds.". . .

Let us then make our conception of the right and wrong of this matter unmistakable. Social relations, one will say, are sacred. True, but civil rights are sacred, also. Hence social relations must not impose upon civil rights nor civil rights impose upon social relations. We must have peace. But for peace to be stable we must have justice. Therefore, for peace, we must find that boundary line between social relations and civil rights, from which the one has no warrant ever to push the other; and, for justice, this boundary must remain ever faithfully the same, no matter whose the social relations are on one side or whose the civil rights are on the other.

Suppose a case. Mr. A. takes a lady, not of his own family, to a concert. Neither one is moved by compulsion or any assertion of right on the part of the other. They have chosen each other's company. Their relation is social. It could not exist without mutual agreement. They are strangers in that city, however, and as they sit in the thronged auditorium and look around them, not one other soul in that house, so far as they can discern, has any social relation with them. But see, now, how impregnable the social relation is. That pair, outnumbered a thousand to one, need not yield a pennyweight of social interchange with any third person unless they so choose. Nothing else in human life is so amply sufficient to protect itself as are social relations. Provided one thing, — that the law will protect every one impartially in his civil rights, one of the foremost of which is that both men and laws shall let us alone to our personal social preferences. If any person, no matter who or what he is, insists

on obtruding himself upon this pair in the concert-hall he can only succeed in getting himself put out. Why? Because he is trying to turn his civil right-to-be-there into a social passport. And even if he makes no personal advances, but his behavior or personal condition is so bad as to obtrude itself offensively upon others, the case is the same; the mistake and its consequences are his. But, on the other hand, should Mr. A. and his companion demand the expulsion of this third person when he had made no advances and had encroached no more on their liberty than they had on his, demanding it simply on the ground that he was their social or intellectual inferior or probably had relatives who were, then the error, no matter who or what he is, would be not his, but theirs, and it would be the equally ungenteel error of trying to turn their social choice into a civil right; and it would be simply increasing the error and its offensiveness, for them to suggest that he be given an equally comfortable place elsewhere in the house providing it must indicate his inferiority. There is nothing comfortable in ignominy, nor is it any evidence of high mind for one stranger to put it upon another.

Now, the principles of this case are not disturbed by any multiplication of the number of persons concerned, or by reading for concert-hall either theater or steamboat or railway station or coach or lecture-hall or steet car or public library, or by supposing the social pair to be English, Turk, Jap, Cherokee, Ethiopian, Mexican, or "American." But note the fact that, even so, Mr. A. and his companion's social relations are, under these rulings, as safe from invasion as they were before; nay, even safer, inasmuch as the true distinction is made publicly clearer, between the social and the civil relations. Mr. A. is just as free to decline every sort of unwelcome social advance, much or little, as ever he was; and as to his own house or estate may eject any one from it, not of his own family or a legal tenant, and give no other reason than that it suits him to do so. Do you not see it now, gentlemen of the other side? Is there anything new in it? Is it not as old as truth itself? Honestly, have you not known it all along? Is it not actually the part of good breeding to know it? You cannot say no. Then why have you charged us with proposing "to break down every distinction between the races," and "to insist on their intermingling in all places and in all relations," when in fact we have not proposed to disturb any distinction between the races which nature has made, or to molest any private or personal relation in life, whatever? Why have you charged us with "moving to forbid all further assortment of the races," when the utmost we have done is to condemn an *arbitrary* assortment of the races, crude and unreasonable, by the stronger race without the consent of the weaker, and in places and relations where no one, exalted or lowly, has any right to dictate to another because of the class he belongs to? We but turn your own words to our use when we say this battery of charges "is as false as it is infamous." But let that go.

Having made it plain that the question has nothing to do with social relations, we see that it is, and is only, a question of *indiscriminative civil rights*. This is what "The Freedman's Case in Equity" advocates from beginning to end, not as a choice which a *race* may either claim or disclaim, but as every citizen's individual yet impersonal right until he personally waives or forfeits it. The issue, we repeat, is not met at all by the assertion that "Neither race wants it." There

is one thing that neither race wants, but even this is not because either of them is one race or another, but simply because they are members of a civilized human community. It is that thing of which our Southern white people have so long had such an absurd fear; neither race, or in other words nobody, wants to see the civil rewards of decency in dress and behavior usurped by the common herd of clowns and ragamuffins. But there is another thing that the colored race certainly does want: the freedom for those of the race who can to earn the indiscriminative and unchallenged *civil — not social* — rights of gentility by the simple act of being genteel. This is what we insist the best intelligence of the South is willing — in the interest of right, and therefore of both races — to accord. But the best intelligence is not the majority, and the majority, leaning not upon the equities, but the traditional sentiments of the situation, charge us with "theory" and "sentiment" and give us their word for it that "Neither race wants it."

Why, that is the very same thing we used to say about slavery! Where have these traditionists been the last twenty years? Who, that lived in the South through those days, but knows that the darker race's demand from the first day of the Reconstruction era to its last, was, "If you *will not give us* undivided participation in civil rights, *then and in that case* you must give us equal separate enjoyment of them"; and from the close of Reconstruction to this day the only change in its expression has been to turn its imperative demand into a supplication. This was the demand, this is the supplication of American citizens seeking not even their civil rights entire, but their civil rights mutilated to accommodate not our public rights but our private tastes. And how have we responded?

Has the separate accommodation furnished them been anywhere nearly equal to ours? Not one time in a thousand. Has this been for malice? Certainly not. But we have unconsciously — and what people in our position would not have made the same oversight? — allowed ourselves to be carried off the lines of even justice by our old notion of every white man holding every negro to a menial status.

Would our friends on the other side of the discussion say they mean only, concerning these indiscriminative civil rights, "Neither race wants them *now*"? This would but make bad worse. For two new things have happened to the colored race in these twenty years; first, a natural and spontaneous assortment has taken place within the race itself along scales of virtue and intelligence, knowledge and manners; so that by no small fraction of their number the wrong of treating the whole race alike is more acutely felt than ever it was before; and, second, a long, bitter experience has taught them that "equal accommodations, but separate" means, generally, accommodations of a conspicuously ignominious inferiority. Are these people opposed to an arrangement that would give them instant release from organized and legalized incivility? — For that is what a race distinction in civil relations is when it ignores intelligence and decorum. . . .

But they have yet one last fancied stronghold. They say, "The *interest* of both races is against it"; that is, against a common participation in their civil rights; and that it is, rather, in favor of a separate enjoyment of them. Now, there are people — but their number is steadily growing less — who would mean by this merely that the interest of both races is against common participation because *they* are against it and have made separate participation the price of peace.

But the gentlemen whom we have in view in this paper, though they must confess their lines often imply this, give a reason somewhat less offensive in its intention. They say common participation means common sociality, and common sociality, race-amalgamation. Have we not just used their own facts to show conclusively that this is not what occurs? Yet these two reasons, so called, are actually the only ones that scrutiny can find in all the utterances pledging these gentlemen to "the exactest justice and the fullest equity." Nay, there is another; we must maintain, they say, "the clear and unmistakable domination of the white race in the South." — Why, certainly we must! and we must do it honestly and without tampering with anybody's natural rights; and we can do it! But why do they say we must do it? Because "character, intelligence, and property" belong preeminently to the white race, and "character, intelligence, and property" have "the right to rule." So, as far as the reasoning is sincere, they are bound to mean that not merely being white entails that right, but the possession of "character, intelligence, and property." And the true formula becomes "the clear and unmistakable domination" of "character, intelligence, and property" "in the South." But if this be the true doctrine, as who can deny it is? then why — after we have run the color line to suit ourselves through all our truly social relations — why need we usurp the prerogative to run it so needlessly through civil rights, also? It is widely admitted that we are vastly the superior race in everything — as a race. But is every colored man inferior to every white man in character, intelligence, and property? Is there no "responsible and steadfast element" at all among a people who furnish 16,000 schoolteachers and are assessed for $91,-

000,000 worth of taxable property? Are there no poor and irresponsible whites? So, the color line and the line of character, intelligence, and property frequently cross each other. Then tell us, gentlemen, which are you really for; the color line, or the line of character, intelligence, and property that divides between those who have and those who have not "the right to rule"? You dare not declare for an inflexible color line; such an answer would shame the political intelligence of a Russian. . . .

The case is before the reader. The points of fact made in our November paper — the privations suffered by the colored people in their matters of civil rights — have been met with feeble half-denials equivalent to admissions by opponents in controversy too engrossed with counter statements and arguments, that crumble at the touch, to attend to a statement of facts. In the end they stand thus: As to churches, there is probably not a dozen in the land, if one, "colored" or "white," where a white person is not at least professedly welcome to its best accommodations; while the colored man though he be seven-eighths white, is shut up, on the ground that "his race" prefers it, to the poor and often unprofitable appointments of the "African" church, whether he like it best or not, unless he is ready to accept without a murmur distinctions that mark him, in the sight of the whole people, as one of a despised caste and that follow him through the very sacraments. As to schooling, despite the fact that he is today showing his eager willingness to accept separate schools for his children wherever the white man demands the separation, yet both his children and the white man's are being consigned to illiteracy wherever they are too few and poor to form separate schools. In some mountainous parts of

Kentucky there is but one colored school district in a *county*. In railway travel the colored people's rights are tossed from pillar to post with an ever-varying and therefore more utterly indefensible and intolerable capriciousness. In Virginia they may ride exactly as white people do and in the same cars. In a neighboring State, a white man may ride in the "ladies' car," while a colored man of exactly the same dress and manners — nay, his wife or daughter — must ride in the notorious "Jim Crow car," unprotected from smokers and dram-drinkers and lovers of vile language. "In South Carolina," says the Charleston "News and Courier," on the other hand, "respectable colored persons who buy first-class tickets on any railroad ride in the first-class cars as a right, and their presence excites no comment on the part of their white fellow-passengers. It is a great deal pleasanter to travel with respectable and well-behaved colored people than with unmannerly and ruffianly white men." In Alabama the majority of the people have not made this discovery, at least if we are to believe their newspapers. In Tennessee the law *requires* the separation of all first-class passengers by race with equal accommodations for both; thus waiving the old plea of decency's exigencies and forcing upon American citizens adjudged to be first-class passengers an alienism that has thrown away its last shadow of an excuse. But this is only the law, and the history of the very case alluded to by our traditionist friends, in which a colored woman gained damages for being compelled to accept inferior accommodation or none for a first-class ticket, is the history of an outrage so glaring that only a person blinded to the simplest rights of human beings could cite it in such a defense.

A certain daily railway train was supplied, according to the law, with a smok-ing-car, and two first-class cars, one for colored and one for whites. The two first-class cars were so nearly of a kind that they were exchangeable. They generally kept their relative positions on the track; but the "ladies' car" of the morning trip became the "colored car" of the return, afternoon trip, and *vice versâ*. But the rules of the colored car were little re-garded. Men, white and black, were sometimes forbidden, sometimes allowed, to smoke and drink there. Says the court, "The evidence is abundant to show that the rule excluding smoking from that car was but a nominal one, that it was often disregarded, that white passengers un-derstood it to be a nominal rule, and that adequate means were not adopted to secure the same first-class and orderly passage to the colored passengers occu-pying that car as was accorded to the passengers in the rear car. Nor was the separation of the classes of the passengers complete. There is no evidence tending to show that the white passengers were excluded from the car assigned to col-ored passengers, and it appears that whenever the train was unusually crowded it was expected that the excess of white passengers would ride, as they then did ride, in the forward one of the two first-class cars. So, too, it appeared that persons of color, of whom the plain-tiff was one, had several times occupied seats in the rear car." A certain "person of lady-like appearance and deportment," one day in September, 1883, got aboard this train with a first-class ticket. She knew the train, and that, as the court states it, "in the rear car . . . quiet and good order were to so great an extent the rule that it was rarely if ever that any passenger gave annoyance by his con-duct to his fellow-passengers." In the colored car there was at least one col-ored man smoking, and one white man whom she saw to be drunk. She entered the rear car and sat down, no one object-ing. She was the only colored person there. The conductor, collecting his tick-ets, came to her. He was not discon-certed. Not long previously he had for-bidden another colored person to ride in that car, who must also have been "of lady-like appearance and deportment," for when he saw this one he "supposed her to be the same person . . . intention-ally violating the defendant's (Rail-road's) rules and *seeking to annoy his other passengers.*" Twice they exchanged polite request and refusal to leave the car; and then, in full presence of all those "other passengers" whom this person of lady-like appearance and deportment was erroneously suspected of "seeking to annoy," there occurred a thing that ought to make the nation blush. The conductor laid hands upon this defenseless woman, whose infraction of a rule was interfering neither with the running of the road, the collection of fares, nor the comfort of passengers, and "by force removed her from the seat and carried her out of the car. When near the door of the car the plaintiff promised that she would then, if permitted, leave the car rather than be forcibly ejected; but the conductor, as he says, told her that her consent came too late, and continued to remove her forcibly. On reaching the platform of the car, plaintiff left the train." Judgment was given for the plaintiff. But the point was carefully made that she would have been without any grievance if the "col-ored car" had only been kept first-class. In other words, for not providing sepa-rate first-class accommodations, five hun-dred dollars damages; for laying violent hands upon a peaceable, lady-like, and unprotected woman, nothing; and noth-ing for requiring such a one publicly to sit apart from passengers of the same grade under a purely ignominious distinction. What! not ignominious? Fancy the passenger a white lady, choosing, for reasons of her own, to sit in a first-class "colored car"; infringing, if you please, some rule; but paying her way, and causing no one any inconvenience, unsafety, or delay. Imagine her, on insisting upon her wish to stay, drawn from her seat by force, and lifted and carried out by a black conductor, telling her as he goes that her offer to walk out comes too late. If this is not ignominy, what is it? To the commission and palliation of such unmanly deeds are we driven by our attempts to hold under our own arbitrary dictation others' rights that we have no moral right to touch, rights that in ourselves we count more sacred than property and dearer than life.

But we must not tarry. If we turn to the matter of roadside refreshment what do we see? Scarcely a dozen railroad refreshment-rooms from the Rio Grande to the Potomac — is there one? — where the weary and hungry colored passenger, be he ever so perfect in dress and behavior, can snatch a hasty meal in the presence of white guests of any class whatever, though in any or every one of them he or she can get the same food, and eat with the same knife, fork, and plate that are furnished to white strangers, if only he or she will take a menial's attitude and accept them in the kitchen. Tennessee has formally "abrogated the rule of the common law" in order to make final end of "any right in favor of any such person so refused admission" to the enjoyment of an obvious civil right which no public host need ever permit any guest to mistake for a social liberty. As to places of public amusement, the gentlemen who say that "each [race] gets the same accommodation for the same money," sim-

ply — forget. The statement comes from Atlanta. But, in fact, in Atlanta, in Georgia, in the whole South, there is scarcely a place of public amusement — except the cheap museums, where there are no seated audiences — in which a colored man or woman, however unobjectionable personally, can buy, at any price, any but a second — sometimes any but a third or fourth class accommodation. During a day's stay in Atlanta lately, the present writer saw many things greatly to admire; many inspiring signs of thrift, stability, virtue, and culture. Indeed, where can he say that he has not seen them, in ten Southern States lately visited? And it is in contemplation of these evidences of greatness, prosperity, safety, and the desire to be just, that he feels constrained to ask whether it must be that in the principal depot of such a city the hopeless excommunication of every person of African tincture from the civil rewards of gentility must be advertised by three signs at the entrances of three separate rooms, one for "Ladies," one for "Gentlemen," and the third a "Colored waiting room"? Visiting the principal library of the city, he was eagerly assured, in response to inquiry, that no person of color would be allowed to draw out books; and when a colored female, not particularly tidy in dress, came forward to return a book and draw another, it was quickly explained that she was merely a servant and messenger for some white person. Are these things necessary to — are they consistent with — an exalted civilization founded on equal rights and the elevation of the masses? . . .

Is it not wonderful? A hundred years we have been fearing to do entirely right lest something wrong should come of it; fearing to give the black man an equal chance with us in the race of life lest we might have to grapple with the vast,

vague afrite of Amalgamation; and in all
this hundred years, with the enemies of
slavery getting from us such names as
negrophiles, negro-worshipers, and mis-
cegenationists; and while we were claiming to hold ourselves rigidly separate
from the lower race in obedience to a
natal instinct which excommunicated
them both socially and civilly; just in
proportion to the rigor, the fierceness,
and the injustice with which this excommunication from the common rights of
man has fallen upon the darker race, has
amalgamation taken place. Look — we
say again — at the West Indies. Then
turn and look at those regions of our
common country that we have been used
to call the nests of fanaticism: Philadelphia, Boston, Plymouth Church, and the
like. . . . Look at Bera, Kentucky, where
every kind thing contrivable that, according to our old ideas, could destroy a white
man's self-respect and "spoil a nigger" has
been practiced. What is the final fact?
Amalgamation? Miscegenation? Not at
all. . . . How have they been kept apart?
by law? By fierce conventionality? By
instinct? No! It was because they *did
not* follow instinct, but the better dictates of reason and the ordinary natural
preferences of like for like. But, it is
sometimes asked, admitting this much,
will not undivided civil relations tend
eventually — say after a few centuries —

to amalgamation? Idle question! Will
it help the matter to withhold men's
manifest rights? What can we do better
for the remotest future than to be just in
the present and leave the rest to the
Divine Rewarder of nations that walk
uprightly?

*"The Silent South" was almost a Parthian
shot. During the same month in which
it appeared, Cable found a new home
in Northampton, Massachusetts, and before the end of the next month he had
located his family there. It could not be
said that Cable was driven from the
South because of his views on the race
problem, but undoubtedly his departure
was urged by the flood of bitterness
which engulfed him and the painful de-
fection of many who had been his closest
friends. He soon had evidence, too, that
public opinion could assume a very practical expression. He found the assess-
ment on his taxable property suddenly
increased, and only the intervention of
his lawyer before the courts secured a
reduction of the sum from $2500 to $225.
(Arlin Turner, George W. Cable, p. 223.)*

*From Northampton, and particularly
during a Southern tour in 1887, he continued to press his case. But the silent
South, if indeed there was a silent South,
would not speak.*

Editor's note.

III. URBAN PATTERNS OF SEGREGATION—
NORTH AND SOUTH

Richard C. Wade: URBAN SEGREGATION DURING SLAVERY

Richard C. Wade, a leading urban historian, published in 1964 a thorough study of slavery in several Southern cities. A portion of this work described a pattern of segregation which predated general emancipation and cast new light upon the source of racial separation in the South. The following selection is from his book, Slavery in the Cities: The South, 1820–1860. *Professor Wade is a member of the faculty of the University of Chicago.*

VIII

WHILE Southern cities increasingly moved to reduce their colored population, both slave and free, they also developed a new system of racial deference more appropriate to urban life than slavery in its traditional form. As the institution of slavery encountered mounting difficulties, and as its control over the blacks weakened, another arrangement was devised which maintained great social distance within the physical proximity of town life. Increasingly public policy tried to separate the races whenever the surveillance of the master was likely to be missing. To do this, the distinction between slave and free Negro was erased; race became more important than legal status; and a pattern of segregation emerged inside the broader framework of the "peculiar institution."

In a sense this tendency was always present, though the reliance on traditional controls obscured its importance. The heart of the established system was, of course, the subordination of the slave to his owner. The wide discretion vested in the master made day-to-day discipline almost a private matter. But in the cities a public etiquette was needed to govern the relations of races when the blacks were beyond the supervision of their owners. Increasingly that etiquette required the separation of black and white without regard to legal status. Beginning in only a few areas, the arrangement spread to include the most important public aspects of life.

Taverns, restaurants, and hotels were always off-limits to the Negroes. The laws against trading with slaves, of course, covered all these areas, and their location in the business part of town prevented much laxity. Free blacks fell under the same ban, though by custom rather than by law. In public conveyances this discrimination appeared again. Richmond's ordinances, to cite but one case, prohibited Negroes from "driving, using or riding in any Hackney coach or other carriage for hire unless in the capacity of a servant." In New Orleans the street railway kept separate cars for blacks. And encroachments on this arrangement met with physical exclusion. In 1833, for instance, when "certain colored persons wishing to go to the lake, took possession of the cars appropriated to white people," the conductor evicted them.

Public grounds, however, presented an even clearer case. Savannah's 1827 ordinances, for example, excluded "negroes, mulattoes, or other colored persons" from "the public promenade in South Broad street, or on that leading from thence to the Hospital." And the preamble said why: "for the purpose of protecting the Citizens while engaged in recreation upon the Public Walks, from molestation or intrusion of improper persons." A section of Richmond's Negro code was entitled "What place slaves not to Walk or be in." The segregated areas included "the grounds adjacent to the City Spring, City Hall, or Athenaeum," as well as "any of the places known as city grounds" and "any public burying ground for white persons." The law relented if the slave accompanied his owner as employer, but the prohibition of free blacks was absolute.

Charleston's regulations kept colored people off the "enclosure of the Garden at White Point" and forbade them "to walk on the East or South Batteries." If attending white children, and if they had a ticket, slaves could enter. Even this variation, however, brought criticism. "It now takes from four to two wenches, *with their attendants,* to take one baby in the air," one white wrote indignantly, while taxpayers are "jostled by a succession of darkies" each of whom has "a detachment of 'little niggers' at her heels."

These measures simply excluded the blacks without providing alternative facilities. It was otherwise in the case of jails, hospitals, and cemeteries. Here the separation was careful and complete, if sometimes painfully contrived. Also, wherever Negroes shared public build-

ings with whites their quarters were set apart. The division was sometimes by room, at other times by floor. But in every case the segregation was clear and unmistakable.

Prisons presented few problems. Either the blacks had a special jail or they were assigned to a designated section of the same building. Some separate jails had the whipping post in a nearby yard; others, such as Charleston's, adjoined workhouses where colored inmates toiled on tough tasks or kept the treadmill going. When gangs were sent to work on the street or other public projects, officials maintained the same distinction. The New Orleans city council was so anxious in this regard that it furnished different colored clothes for Negro and white prisoners employed on municipal projects.

The same principle governed the organization of poorhouses. The care of the indigent slave, of course, fell to the owner, but free Negroes were the city's responsibility. If the "mandate of the law, the counsel of true wisdom and policy, as well as the dictates of justice and humanity," made them "the fit and rightful objects of poor relief," as a Charleston report observed, it was also "conceded" that they should be "provided for in a place different and separated from . . . the white poor." "The distinction of castes must be strictly and broadly pursued in slaveholding communities," the committee explained. In Baltimore, where the numbers were much greater, a similar practice developed. In the 1830's some mixing occurred because of a continuing space shortage. By 1841, however, the trustees could say that "the colored and white inmates are in general kept separate from each other." Two years later, a new building permitted the removal of white women from the female yard, and thus the Negroes were left with a "comfortable hospital and eating room . . . instead of their being confined exclusively to the garret rooms of the west wing."

Hospitals, too, maintained the pattern. It was most obvious when the institution was initially built for slaves exclusively. Each city had at least one of these. But most also established hospitals which admitted both races to separate quarters and facilities. Usually a wing, or in the case of Louisville, the basement, was set aside for the blacks. Even in times of emergency, when additional structures were taken over for hospital use, health officials did not abandon the practice.

Cultural and recreational enterprises were also segregated when they did not exclude Negroes entirely. Theaters provided special galleries for colored persons which were often approached through special entrances. Lyell found the upper tiers of boxes at the New Orleans Opera House assigned to Negroes. Another visitor reported, "Some of them were pointed out to me as very wealthy; but no money can admit them to the pit, or to the boxes." Others, like Thomas L. Nichols, put a different construction on the segregation, when he referred to the "portion of the house devoted to ladies and gentlemen of colour" where "no common white trash was allowed to intrude." But the fact of separation had been part of official policy since the beginning. As early as 1816 an ordinance established the practice: "It shall not be lawful for any white person to occupy any of the places set apart for people of color; and the latter are likewise forbidden to occupy any of those reserved for white persons, at any public exposition or theatre."

On the stage, of course, no intrusion was permitted. When a Northern newspaper reported that a colored actress had performed in New Orleans, the *Bee* retorted indignantly: "We beg leave to contradict and unequivocally this remark. No negress ever has been, or ever will be permitted to appear on the stage of New Orleans. We are a slave-holding state, and whatever may be the pretended philanthropy of our Northern brethren in relation to our conduct, we possess too much self-respect to submit to any such degrading exhibition." The prohibition on reading and writing, of course, put libraries off-limits.

Negroes remained as segregated in death as in life. Funerals increasingly became wholly colored affairs. The law usually required a white minister at the service, and the master and the family sometimes attended, but a petition by Richmond's blacks to the state legislature indicated the reality. The Negroes noted that a new statute, passed in 1832, prohibited slaves and free Negroes from officiating at funerals. As a consequence, they lamented, "many coloured human beings are inter'd like brutes, their relatives and friends being unable to procure white ministers to perform the usual ceremony in the burial of the dead." Eleven clergymen joined in the memorial arguing that the "pressing engagements of white ministers left no time for this function."

The body was finally interred in a segregated cemetery. Sometimes a congregation would set aside space in its church yard for colored members. No doubt, too, though the evidence is scarce, a faithful slave would on rare occasions be buried in the master's plot. But the bulk of urban Negroes, slave and free, rested ultimately in places confined to their own race. Every city maintained at least one extensive "burial ground for negroes," and most churches kept separate cemeteries for black and white. A Charleston directory for 1856 lists fifteen colored graveyards, two owned by the town, one by the Brown Fellowship Society, and the rest by Negro or white congregations. Nowhere else were there so many, but everywhere the distinction was maintained. And New Orleans, with mathematical precision, divided its facilities into three parts: one-half for whites, one-quarter for slaves, and one-quarter for free blacks.

IX

Religious organizations quickly developed segregated facilities without the help of municipal officials and the law. Nearly all Protestant denominations, especially those with large black contingents, either put their colored members in separate galleries during regular services or established special churches for them. This arrangement covered not only Sunday gatherings but prayer meetings during the week and Bible classes as well. The system, however, stemmed less from white design than Negro preference, for whenever the opportunity appeared colored worshippers patronized their own congregations. A Savannah preacher recorded the normal experience in 1819: "There was one side of the gallery [in his church] appropriated for their use, and it was always the most thinly seated part of the church; while there were two respectably large colored churches in the city, with their pastor, and deacons, and sacraments, and discipline, all of their own."

Colored churches, of course, reflected the tendency toward segregation even more clearly. Distrusted by whites, enthusiastically supported by Negroes, they represented the ambiguity of race relations under slavery. Whites developed elaborate devices to keep the races apart

in public places and to seal off their own slaves from others in private life; but religious activity fell between these situations. Masters, often considering it a family affair, sought a compromise under one roof. Negroes, on the other hand, finding social as well as spiritual satisfaction by themselves, flocked to separate congregations. Except for some Catholic churches and a few Protestant ones, this combination made Sunday morning one of the most segregated moments of the week.

Slaves were excluded from schools by the legislation against teaching them to read and write, but the pattern of segregation applied to free blacks. Not only could they not attend white classes, but they had to make their own arrangements for education. Even these schools had uncertain careers, being subject to police interference and legal prohibitions as well as financial difficulties. After the Vesey episode, the Charleston grand jury wanted to remove all Negro teachers in private schools, which would have shut them down altogether. "As the Blacks are most carefully excluded from all schools kept by *white* persons, where their persons would be considered as a sort of contamination both by the master and scholars," an English visitor observed, "this bill of the Grand Jury will deprive them at once of all instruction." Indeed, he concluded, "Although they do not avow it (for even the most hardened are sometime sensible to public shame)," it was "their real object and intention." If some slaves managed to bootleg a little learning in a free colored school, no black was ever knowingly admitted to a white one.

This exclusion did not, however, exempt Baltimore's large free Negro population from paying the public school tax. As early as 1839, 55 colored leaders asked the mayor to grant them relief, since "coloured people are not at all interested in the public schools directly or indirectly." Failing in that, five years later they asked for "two schools in different sections of the city" for their own children. In 1850, 90 Negroes were joined by 126 whites in another petition. Noting that the blacks "are taxed for the support of public schools, into which, for obvious reasons, their children cannot be admitted," it argued that "the true instinct of the white population, as well as the colored, will be promoted by the instruction of the children . . . in such elements of learning as may prepare them . . . with usefulness and respectability, [for] those humble stations in the community to which they are confined by the necessities of their situation." The solution lay in establishing schools for the 20,000 Negro residents. The city refused on the ground that the state would withdraw money from Baltimore's "school fund" if any went to Negro schools.

x

Law and custom sanctioned the segregation of races in public places and accommodations as well as in churches and schools. To disentangle white and black in employment and housing was a different matter. Yet the significant fact is that such a separation took place increasingly often in the last few decades before the Civil War. Under the pressure of white craftsmen, Negroes were pushed out of one line of work after another. With the weakening of the reins of slavery, bondsmen found housing away from their owners and generally in areas of accumulating colored population. Both movements were far from complete, but the tendency was unmistakable.

In employment the clearest manifestation of segregation was the exclusion of blacks, slave and free, from the better jobs. A memorial of Charleston's City Council to the state legislature expressed both the difficulties and the objects of the policy. Noting that "slavery is so interwoven with the constitution of our Society that even if our interests permitted it would be impossible to eradicate it," the petitioners argued that it was "necessary to fix as far as possible the grade of employments" for slaves and "to exclude them by Legislative enactment from all others." Charleston's own ordinances prohibited teaching slaves "in any mechanic or handicraft trade," though the wording was vague and its enforcement almost impossible.

In Savannah the restrictions were more precise. No Negro could be apprenticed "to the trade of Carpenter, Mason, Bricklayer, Barber or any other Mechanical Art or Mystery." Later, cabinetmaker, painter, blacksmith, tailor, cooper, and butcher were added to the list. Georgia excluded blacks from "being mechanics or masons, from making contracts for the erection . . . or repair of buildings." Though no two cities had the same categories, all tried to keep colored workers out of the higher skills. The fact that practice often belied the law simply underlined the significance of the intent.

If slaves and blacks were still found in many of the better crafts in 1860, they had been pushed out of many of the lesser-skilled jobs. In Baltimore whites took the carting and draying business from them by 1830. A few years later, a visitor could report that "the Irish and other foreigners are, to a considerable extent, taking the place of colored laborers and of domestic servants." In 1823 the City Council of New Orleans directed the mayor "to hire white labor for the city works, in preference to negroes." Two decades later, some prominent citizens there described the extent of the attrition: "Ten years ago, say they, all the draymen of New Orleans, a numerous class, and the cabmen, were colored. Now they are nearly all white. The servants of the great hotels were formerly of the African, now they are of the European race." Even in the home, the displacement occurred with the customary racial rationale. "We have all times spoken against the impropriety of having white and black servants in homes in the South," the *Richmond Enquirer* explained, "especially so in any capacity where slaves or negroes may be inclined to consider themselves on a par of equality with white servants."

John S. C. Abbott, who toured the South in 1859, found this tendency pronounced everywhere. In Mobile, for instance, he was "surprised to see how effectually free labor seems to have driven slave labor from the wharves and streets." The Irish and Germans, he noted, did the outside work, while white girls moved into domestic service. When he saw New Orleans, he commented, though no doubt with exaggeration, that "hardly a colored face is to be seen on the levee, and the work is done by the Germans and the Irish. . . . Indeed, now, New Orleans and Mobile seem but little more like slave cities than do Philadelphia and New York."

Though the process varied in Dixie's cities and Negroes hung on in many skills, "job busting" became a normal tactic for the growing white labor force faced with traditional colored employment practices. As the black population dropped, white newcomers moved in and took over craft after craft. Occasionally accompanied by violence and usually with official sanction, slave and free colored workers were shunted into the most menial and routine chores. In 1830 Negroes, both slave and free, had been used

in a wide variety of employments; by 1860 the number of possibilities had shrunk markedly. The movement toward segregation, so noticeable in other aspects of urban life, was rapidly invading employment.

In housing the same trend was perceptible, though less advanced. The spread of the "living out" system, both in its legal and irregular form, gave slaves some choice of residence. Since the urge to leave the enclosure reflected the freedom from surveillance it entailed, slaves sought spots as removed from whites as possible. For most this meant a retreat to the outer edges of the city or beyond the municipal line altogether. There was seldom any escape from all whites, but there were parts of town with clusters of colored inhabitants. By the 'forties and 'fifties it was apparent in most places that Negroes were settling on the periphery of the cities.

Savannah is a good illustration of this process. The central portion had always been the commercial heart of town. Immediately around it and stretching southward, the substantial and the wealthy built their houses. The best addresses bore the names of eight or ten squares directly away from the wharf toward Forsyth Park. The western and southern edges became the sites for the low-income whites and increasingly for the free colored as well. As slaves moved away from the master's yards, they headed for these areas.

The 1848 census, which listed slaves from their actual place of residence rather than from their master's addresses, revealed the concentrations. Old Oglethorpe Ward on the west had 1327 Negroes to 999 whites. In the same place there were only five brick houses to 451 wooden ones. To the east, Carpenter's Row, Trustees Gardens, and Gilmerville showed the same tendency with fewer

numbers. There 300 blacks lived with
182 whites; none of the 127 houses was
brick. Significantly enough, Currytown
on the southeast edge of the city showed
the same characteristics — Negro majori-
ties and wooden dwellings. Elsewhere
in Savannah, the figures ran the other
way, with white preponderance and
large numbers of brick homes.

The movement to the periphery was
increasingly common, though in some
towns colored concentrations grew up
more haphazardly in small enclaves or
strips in out-of-the-way places. And the
centers of Negro life, formal and informal, followed the people. Colored
churches, especially those established
after 1840, sought locations in these
neighborhoods. Grocery stores and dram
shops, too, settled there. Even the cemeteries were put near the living. In
Savannah's case, for example, four Negro
churches, three Baptist, and one Methodist, were on the west side, while another
served the east side. The central city had
none. Of 174 "grocers" 101 did business
in the outer residential wards, West
Broad alone accommodating 19. In
Charleston the convergence was on the
northern border and the Neck beyond.

In no case did anything like full residential segregation emerge. Few streets,
much less blocks, were solidly black.
Everywhere some whites occupied nearby
dwellings. Still the inclination to cluster
here, to concentrate there, was more
marked by 1860 than in 1820. The separation apparent in other areas of life
was slowly insinuated into housing.

Thus, even before slavery had been
abolished, a system of segregation had
grown up in the cities. Indeed, the whites
thought some such arrangement was necessary if they were to sustain their traditional supremacy over the Negroes. The
countryside provided enough room to
give meaning to racial separation. The
master could be physically quite removed
from his blacks, though sharing the same
plantation or farm. And together both
were isolated from others. In cities these
spatial relationships were quite different.
Both races were thrown together; they
encountered each other at every corner,
they rubbed elbows at every turn; they
divided up, however inequitably, the limited space of the town site. Segregation
sorted people out by race, established a
public etiquette for their conduct, and
created social distance where there was
proximity. Urban circumstances produced this system long before the de-
struction of slavery itself.

Of course, the complete separation of
races was impossible in the city, and the
practice differed from place to place. In
some towns, public conveyances remained mixed; in others Negroes were
not excluded from all public grounds;
in still others housing continued scram-
bled. Yet every city developed its own
arrangement expressed in the contrived
separation of colored and white in count-
less ways. Though never total, the segregation was so extensive that Negroes
were never permitted to forget their inferior position.

Leon F. Litwack: SEGREGATION IN THE ANTEBELLUM NORTH

In 1961 Professor Litwack printed his detailed study of the Negro in the North before the Civil War. The following selection from North of Slavery *indicates the degree of racial separation which he found. Dr. Litwack is a professor of history on the faculty of the University of California, Berkeley.*

WHILE statutes and customs circumscribed the Negro's political and judicial rights, extralegal codes — enforced by public opinion — relegated him to a position of social inferiority and divided northern society into "Brahmins and Pariahs."[1] In virtually every phase of existence, Negroes found themselves systematically separated from whites. They were either excluded from railway cars, omnibuses, stagecoaches, and steamboats or assigned to special "Jim Crow" sections; they sat, when permitted, in secluded and remote corners of theaters and lecture halls; they could not enter most hotels, restaurants, and resorts, except as servants; they prayed in "Negro pews" in the white churches, and if partaking of the sacrament of the Lord's Supper, they waited until the whites had been served the bread and wine. Moreover, they were often educated in segregated schools, punished in segregated prisons, nursed in segregated hospitals, and buried in segregated cemeteries. Thus, one observer concluded, racial prejudice "haunts its victim wherever he goes — in the hospitals where humanity suffers — in the churches where it kneels to God — in the prisons where it expiates its offences — in the graveyards where it sleeps the last sleep."[2]

To most northerners, segregation constituted not a departure from democratic principles, as certain foreign critics alleged, but simply the working out of natural laws, the inevitable consequence of the racial inferiority of the Negro. God and Nature had condemned the blacks to perpetual subordination. Within the context of ante bellum northern thought and "science," this was not an absurd or hypocritical position. Integration, it was believed, would result in a disastrous mixing of the races. "We were taught by our mothers," a New York congressman explained, "to avoid all communications with them" so that "the theorists and utopians never would be able to bring about an amalgamation."[3]

The education of northern youths — at

[1] Abdy, *Journal of a Residence and Tour*, I, 44; Chambers, *Things as They Are in America*, pp. 354–58; Henry B. Fearon, *Sketches of America* (London, 1818), pp. 60–61, 168–69.

[2] Gustave De Beaumont, *Marie, or Slavery in the United States* (tr. by Barbara Chapman, Stanford, 1958), pp. 66, 75–76; *Men and Things in America*, pp. 179–81; [James Boardman], *America, and the Americans* (London, 1833), p. 311; Chambers, *American Slavery and Colour*, pp. 131–35; Francis J. Grund, *Aristocracy in America* (2 vols.; London, 1839), I, 177–78; [Thomas Hamilton], *Men and Manners in America* (2 vols.; London, 1834), I, 93–99; Charles Mackay, *Life and Liberty in America* (2 vols.; London, 1859), II, 41–42; Edward Sullivan, *Rambles and Scrambles in North and South America* (London, 1852), pp. 203–4.

[3] *Appendix to the Congressional Globe*, 30 Cong., 1 sess., p. 581.

Reprinted from *North of Slavery: The Negro in the Free States, 1790–1860,* by Leon F. Litwack by permission of The University of Chicago Press. Copyright 1961 by The University of Chicago. The following material is taken from pages 97–100 and 103–12. In 1965 The University of Chicago Press published a paperback edition of this volume in its Phoenix series.

home and in school — helped to perpetuate popular racial prejudices and stereotypes and to confirm the Negro in his caste position. In 1837, for example, a Boston Negro minister discussed the origins of racial attitudes in the younger generation. As children, whites were warned to behave or "the old nigger will carry you off," and they were reprimanded as being "worse than a little *nigger.*" Later, parents encouraged their children to improve themselves, lest they "be poor or ignorant as a *nigger*" or "have no more credit than a *nigger.*" Finally, teachers frequently punished their students by sending them to the "nigger-seat" or by threatening to put them in a Negro class. Such training, the Negro minister concluded, had been "most disastrous upon the mind of the community; having been instructed from youth to look upon a black man in no other light than a slave."[4] Under such circumstances, white adults could hardly be expected to afford Negroes equal political and social rights.

Northerners drew the Negro stereotype in the image of his political, economic, and social degradation and constantly reminded him of his inferiority. Newspapers and public places prominently displayed cartoons and posters depicting his alleged physical deformities and poking fun at his manners and customs. The minstrel shows, a popular form of entertainment in the ante bellum North, helped to fix a public impression of the clownish, childish, carefree, and irresponsible Negro and prompted one Negro newspaper to label these black-face imitators as "the filthy scum of white society, who have stolen from us a complexion denied to them by nature, in which to make money, and pander to the corrupt taste of their fellow-citizens."[5] Nevertheless, the minstrel shows, newspapers, and magazines combined to produce a Negro stereotype that hardly induced northerners to accord this clownish race equal political and social rights. As late as 1860, a group of New York Negroes, in an appeal for equal suffrage, complained bitterly that every facet of northern opinion had been turned against them. "What American artist has not caricatured us?" they asked. "What wit has not laughed at us in our wretchedness? has not ridiculed and condemned us? Few, few, very few."[6]

In addition to persistent public reminders of their physical and mental inferiority, Negroes frequently complained that they had to endure "abusive epithets" and harassment when walking through white areas or shopping in white stores. In passing a group of white men, "ten chances to one" there would be a "sneer or snigger, with characteristic accompanying remarks." Children often tormented them in the streets and hurled insulting language and objects at them.[7] "There appears to be a fixed determination on the part of our oppressors in this country," a Negro wrote in 1849, "to destroy every vestige of self-respect, self-possession, and manly independence left in the colored people; and when all things else have failed, or may be inconvenient, a resort to brow-beating, bully-

---

4 Hosea Easton, *A Treatise on the Intellectual Character, and Civil and Political Condition of the Colored People of the United States; and the Prejudice Exercised Towards Them* (Boston, 1837), pp. 40–41, 43.

5 *North Star*, October 27, 1848.

6 Aptheker (ed.), *Documentary History*, p. 456.

7 Easton, *A Treatise*, p. 41; *North Star*, March 30, 1849; Abdy, *Journal of a Residence and Tour*, III, 206–7; Mrs. Felton, *American Life: A Narrative of Two Years' City and Country Residence in the United States* (London, 1842), p. 58.

ragging, and ridicule is at once and at all times had."[8]

* * *

By the 1840's, an increasing number of northern Negroes refused to accept passively their assigned place in society. In addition to agitating for equal suffrage, judicial, and educational rights, they sought to break down those barriers which excluded them from public places and vehicles or which segregated them in Jim Crow sections. Experience had taught the Negro that only constant pressure for immediate changes, rather than a passive trust in gradualism, would produce results. Accordingly, Negroes secured the assistance of white abolitionists, formed independent organizations, published several newspapers, and achieved some remarkable progress toward racial equality. The success of their agitation varied from state to state, but nowhere was it more vividly demonstrated than in Massachusetts.

After 1821, the political position of the Massachusetts Negro gradually and perceptibly improved. His right to vote and hold office had been generally acknowledged, but such progress had not been made in the economic and social spheres, where Negroes competed with new immigrants for the menial employments and encountered the familiar pattern of segregation, extending from public transportation to the theater. In 1831, Boston's mayor, Harrison Gray Otis, described the Negro inhabitants as "a quiet, inoffensive, and in many respects a useful race," but the "repugnance to intimate social relations with them is insurmountable." Fifteen years later, the state statistician reported that racial prejudice doomed Massachusetts Negroes to economic and social inferiority and accounted for the decrease of their numerical strength in proportion to the whites. On the eve of the Civil War, abolitionist Senator Henry Wilson admitted in Congress that powerful prejudices still existed and that Negroes "with the same intellectual qualities, the same moral qualities, are not in Massachusetts regarded as they would be if they were white men."[9]

Possession of the suffrage, then, did not automatically open the doors of white society. Statutes barred Massachusetts Negroes from intermarrying with whites, and extralegal restrictions segregated them in public places and vehicles. In 1841, the fear of possible mob violence even prompted Boston authorities to place Negro participants in the rear of President William Henry Harrison's funeral procession.[10] Any attempt to secure equal rights for Negroes would first have to arouse public opinion to the undemocratic nature of such distinctions. With this in mind, Massachusetts abolitionists — Negro and white — set out to convince an apathetic and frequently hostile public that a consistent stand against southern slavery involved the full recognition of the rights of local Negroes.

In one of the first issues of *The Liberator*, William Lloyd Garrison launched a campaign to repeal the law barring marriages between Negroes and whites.[11] Abolitionists accompanied an incessant editorial barrage with a continuous flow of petitions to the legislature and placed particular emphasis on the inconsistency of such a statute with the state's traditional hostility to slavery. "So long as Southerners can point to it on her Statute

[8] *North Star,* March 30, 1849.

[9] *Niles' Weekly Register,* XLV (September 14, 1833), 43; Jesse Chickering, *A Statistical View of the Population of Massachusetts, from 1765 to 1840* (Boston, 1846), pp. 155–60; *Congressional Globe,* 35 Cong., 1 sess., p. 1966.
[10] *National Anti-Slavery Standard,* May 20, 1841.
[11] *The Liberator,* January 8, 1831. See also May 7, 1831, January 28, February 11, March 31, 1832, February 5, 1841, February 24, 1843.

Book," John Greenleaf Whittier declared, "the anti-slavery testimony of Massachusetts is shorn of half its strength."[12] Agreeing with this sentiment, a legislative committee concluded that the existence of such a law belied "sentiments which we have heretofore expressed to Congress and to the world on the subject of slavery, for by denying to our colored fellow-citizens any of the privileges and immunities of freemen, we virtually assert their inequality, and justify that theory of negro slavery which represents it as a state of necessary tutelage and guardianship."[13]

The possibility that Massachusetts might actually repeal its ban on interracial marriages drew some bitter comments from both northern and southern newspapers, including a warning that "such alliances will never be tolerated in New England."[14] Some legislators defended the law on the ground that it was not discriminatory because it applied equally to both races; moreover, it recognized certain natural distinctions, "which nothing but the insanity of fanaticism dares to arraign," and prevented a deterioration of the white race.[15] Nevertheless, after more than a decade of agitation, the legislature voted, on February 24, 1843, to repeal the act. Abolitionists hailed the successful campaign as "another staggering blow . . . to the monster prejudice," and Garrison reassured an English correspondent that their object

was not to promote amalgamation but "to establish justice, and vindicate the equality of the human race."[16]

Simultaneously with their attack on the intermarriage ban, abolitionists moved to abolish the Jim Crow railroad cars. Precedents already established in stagecoaches and steamships, as well as the existing state of public opinion, accounted for the assignment of Negroes to special coaches.[17] Josiah Quincy, Jr., president of the Boston and Providence Railroad, recalled that when the Providence road opened the shortest route to New York, "it was found that an appreciable number of the despised race demanded transportation. Scenes of riot and violence took place, and in the then existing state of opinion, it seemed to me that the difficulty could best be met by assigning a special car to our colored citizens."[18] As early as 1838 — only a few years after railroads first came into public use in Massachusetts — Negroes demanded an end to segregation on trains, steamboats, and stagecoaches. By the 1840's, the newspapers frequently reported cases of Negroes' being forcibly removed from railroad cars for refusing to sit in the Jim Crow sections.[19]

The failure to secure a court injunction

[12] *Ibid.*, February 22, 1839.
[13] *Massachusetts House of Representatives, House Report*, No. 46 (March 6, 1840), pp. 7–8; No. 7 (January 19, 1841).
[14] Editorial comment reprinted in *The Liberator*, April 2, May 21, June 11, 1831, February 8, 1839, and in *National Anti-Slavery Standard*, April 1, 1841. For the critical reaction of a Hallowell, Maine, town meeting, see Charles L. Remond to Elizabeth Pease, May 5, 1841, Garrison Papers, Boston Public Library.
[15] *Massachusetts House of Representatives, House Report*, No. 28 (February 25, 1839), p. 10; No. 74 (April 3, 1839).

[16] William Lloyd Garrison to Richard D. Webb, February 28, 1843, Garrison Papers.
[17] For origins of the term "Jim Crow" as applied to separate railroad accommodations, apparently first used in Massachusetts, see Mitford M. Mathews (ed.), *A Dictionary of Americanisms* (2 vols.; Chicago, 1951), I, 906–7. Some examples of stagecoach and steamboat segregation may be found in *Freedom's Journal*, March 23, 1827; *The Liberator*, January 15, December 10, 1831, July 7, August 11, 1832, December 28, 1833, November 30, 1838, September 17, 1841; Abdy, *Journal of a Residence and Tour*, II, 48–49.
[18] Josiah Quincy, Jr., *Figures of the Past* (Boston, 1883), pp. 340–41.
[19] August W. Hanson to Frances Jackson, October 22, 1838, Garrison Papers; *The Liberator*, October 18, 1839, July 2, 9, 23, August 27, October 1, 8, 15, November 5, 12, 1841; *Colored American*, September 25, October 30, 1841.

against such practices prompted Negroes to turn to the legislature for relief. Meanwhile, abolitionists urged their followers to boycott companies which sanctioned segregation and to flood the legislature with petitions. In an effort to arouse public indignation, they pointed out that southern slaveholders, when traveling through the state, were allowed to keep their Negro bondsmen with them in cars which excluded native free Negroes. Therefore, "it is *not* color alone which excluded a man from the best car. The colored person to be excluded must also be *free!!*"[20]

Abolitionist agitation produced the desired effect. In 1842, a joint legislative committee, after conducting hearings, reported that the railroad restrictions violated the Negro's rights as a citizen, conflicted with the state constitution, and "would be an insult to any white man." Since the railroad companies derived corporate privileges from the legislature, the committee recommended a bill which would prohibit any distinctions in accommodations because of descent, sect, or color.[21] Governor Marcus Morton suggested, in the following year, that if any citizens, in railroad cars or elsewhere, sustained injuries because of their descent or color for which no legal redress was available, they should be provided with remedies adequate to their protection in the enjoyment of their just and equal rights."[22]

Such sentiment was not unanimous.

The railroad directors argued that all Massachusetts corporations had been granted the power to make "reasonable and proper" by-laws for the management of their business, and "the established usage and the public sentiment of this community authorize a separation of the blacks from the whites in public places." A Boston newspaper charged that recent legislative proposals, designed to make Massachusetts a "paradise of colored people," had resulted in a sizable increase in Negro immigration. The effect of the proposed railroad bill, the newspaper pointed out, would be to subject passengers "to the hazard of being compelled to sit cheek by jowl with any colored person who may chance to seize upon the adjoining seat." Moreover, a state senator warned, such legislation would not stop at forcing the mixture of Negroes and whites in railroad cars but would subsequently be applied to hotels, religious societies, "and through all the ramifications of society."[23]

The legislature refused to adopt the proposed act. Nevertheless, constant abolitionist pressure, the growing impact of public opinion, and the threat of legislative action prompted the railroad companies to abandon segregation, and only a few cases were reported after 1842. Frederick Douglass, who had frequently been a victim of these restrictions, noted in 1849 that "not a single railroad can be found in any part of Massachusetts, where a colored man is treated and esteemed in any other light than that of a man and a traveler." The abolitionists had scored a significant triumph.[24]

Although so often rebuked for their ignorance, Negroes frequently found it difficult to take advantage of the increas-

[20] *The Liberator,* October 1, November 5, 1841. Two unsuccessful attempts to obtain court action against the railroads are described in *ibid.,* August 6, November 5, 1841.
[21] *Massachusetts Senate, Senate Report,* No. 63 (February 22, 1842). For the testimony of Wendell Phillips and Charles L. Remond before the legislative committee, see *The Liberator,* February 18, 25, 1842.
[22] Marcus Morton to Henry I. Bowditch, October 2, 1843, Garrison Papers.

[23] *The Liberator,* November 5, 1841, February 10, 17, 1843.
[24] *Ibid.,* April 28, 1843, June 8, 1849.

ing opportunities for adult education, particularly the popular lecture presentations of the Lyceum. Lecture-hall managers either refused them admittance or consigned them to remote corners, usually in the balcony. In Boston, where this was apparently not the practice, one Lyceum subscriber protested in the local press that he refused to "carry a lady to a lecture, and compel her to do the penance of sitting cheek by jowl with a negro." In the absence of any restrictions, he warned that the Boston Lyceum, among the first to be established in the United States, would "become nothing more than the patron and upholder of abolition orgies; the auditory consisting of the same class usually found in the third tier and gallery of the theatres."[25] The Boston Lyceum apparently withstood such attacks and managed to survive.

In nearby New Bedford, however, Lyceum authorities in 1845 excluded Negroes from membership and assigned them to gallery seats — after they had once enjoyed the same privileges as whites. This precipitated an immediate reaction. In addition to abolitionist threats to boycott the Lyceum, three prominent lecturers — Ralph Waldo Emerson, Charles Sumner, and Theodore Parker — refused to appear there until the restrictions had been rescinded. Emerson told a Concord abolitionist "that the Lyceum being a popular thing designed for the benefit of all, *particularly* for the most ignorant . . . he should not know how to address an assembly where this class was excluded, and if any were excluded, it should be the cultivated classes."[26] When the Lyceum remained

adamant in its refusal to admit Negroes to membership, abolitionists organized a rival association.[27]

By 1859, a Boston Negro leader could point not only to the frequent presence of his people at popular lectures but also to the actual appearance of Frederick Douglass and other prominent Negro abolitionists on Lyceum platforms. Exclusion and segregation, however, still confronted Negroes in several Boston theaters, and legal action to abolish these restrictions proved largely unsuccessful.[28]

By the eve of the Civil War, Massachusetts Negroes had made considerable progress toward the attainment of full civil rights, but much remained to be done. "Some persons think," a Boston Negro leader remarked in 1860, "that because we have the right to vote, and enjoy the privilege of being squeezed up in an omnibus, and stared out of a seat in a horse-car, that there is less prejudice here than there is farther South." This was only partially true, he continued, for "it is five times as hard to get a house in a good location in Boston as it is in Philadelphia, and it is ten times as difficult for a colored mechanic to get work here as it is in Charleston." Moreover, local restaurants, hotels and theaters continued to exclude the Negro, while at least two amusement places helped to perpetuate existing prejudices through constant caricature and ridicule.[29]

---

[25] *Ibid.*, January 13, 1843.

[26] Mary Brooks to Caroline Weston, March 19, November 24, 1845, Weston Papers; Deborah Weston to Anne Warren Weston, October 1845,

ibid.; Sumner, *Works,* I, 160–62; Zephaniah W. Pease (ed.), *The Diary of Samuel Rodman: A New Bedford Chronicle of Thirty-Seven Years, 1821–1859* (New Bedford, 1927), pp. 269–70; *The Liberator,* October 31, November 28, 1845.

[27] Maria (Weston) Chapman, "An Incident of Anti-Slavery Reform," n.d., Weston Papers; *The Liberator,* December 5, 19, 1845.

[28] Catterall (ed.), *Judicial Cases,* IV, 524, 527–28; Mary C. Crawford, *Romantic Days in Old Boston* (Boston, 1922), p. 249; *The Liberator,* October 30, 1857.

[29] *The Liberator,* March 16, 1860.

Few could deny, however, that in several areas the Negro had at least ceased to be a second-class citizen. He could now vote, hold public office, testify in court, sit as a juror, ride public vehicles, and intermarry with whites. To many observers, especially those from outside the state, it was a rather frightening spectacle: amalgamation had run amuck in the Puritan Commonwealth.[30]

Elsewhere in the North, Negroes met with little success in their efforts to break down segregation. Rather than submit to further harassment on New York City public conveyances, Negroes formed the "Legal Rights Association," deliberately violated company segregation rules, and employed, among others, Chester A. Arthur as legal counsel.[31] The railroad directors replied, however, that public sentiment required separate cars for Negroes and pointed out that Negroes could stand on the front platforms of any cars. In a case involving the expulsion of a Negro woman from a segregated car, the presiding judge instructed the jury that Negroes, "if sober, well behaved, and free from disease," possessed the same rights as whites and could not be excluded by force or violence from public conveyances. The jury convicted the railroad company of negligence and ordered damages paid to the plaintiff.[32] However, one year later — in 1856 — a jury refused to convict a railroad company for ejecting a Negro minister from one of its cars. In a lengthy instruction to the jury, the presiding judge pointed out that common carriers had the right to prescribe reasonable rules and regulations, that they were not obligated to carry particular persons when such action might adversely affect their interests, and that consideration had to be given to "the probable effect upon the capital, business and interests of admitting blacks into their cars indiscriminately with the whites." Moreover, the principles involved in this case could readily be applied to hotel owners, omnibus proprietors "and all others of that description."[33]

When Philadelphia streetcars went into operation in 1858, Negroes could ride only on the front platform. Protesting this practice, one local newspaper charged that Philadelphia was the only northern city which barred Negroes from the public conveyances and that this prevented them from moving to outlying areas where they could secure cleaner and more comfortable homes at cheaper rates. The Philadelphia District Court, however, upheld the restriction as a consequence of the different treatment accorded Negroes and whites, particularly since 1838. Finally, in 1867, a legislative act forbade segregation in public conveyances.[34]

Although the Negro made substantial gains in Massachusetts and scored sporadic successes elsewhere, his general political and social position remained unaltered. By 1860, the North had clearly defined its position on racial relations: white supremacy and social peace required a vigorous separation of blacks and whites and the concentration of po-

[30] *Appendix to the Congressional Globe*, 36 Cong., 1 sess., pp. 284–85.

[31] New York *Daily Times*, August 27, 1855; *Frederick Douglass' Paper*, May 11, September 7, 1855; Leo H. Hirsch, Jr., "The Negro and New York, 1783 to 1865," *Journal of Negro History*, XVI (1931), 426.

[32] New York *Daily Times*, May 29, 1855; *Frederick Douglass' Paper*, July 28, 1854, March 2, 1855.

[33] New York *Daily Times*, December 18, 20, 1856.

[34] *The Liberator*, September 21, 1860; Turner, *Negro in Pennsylvania*, pp. 197–98; *A Brief Narrative of the Struggle for the Rights of the Colored People of Philadelphia in the City Railway Cars* (Philadelphia, 1867).

litical and judicial power in the hands of the superior race — the Caucasian. "The result," an English traveler observed, "is a singular social phenomenon. We see, in effect, two nations — one white and another black — growing up together within the same political circle, but never mingling on a principle of equality."[35]

[35] Chambers, *Things as They Are in America,* p. 357.

Benjamin H. Hunt: WHY SEGREGATION IN POSTWAR PHILADELPHIA

SOME remarks lately communicated to the New York Anti-Slavery Standard, on the continued exclusion of colored people from our street cars, leave the impression that no efforts have been made here to procure for this class of people admission to these cars. This is incorrect. It will be found on inquiry, that a Committee, consisting of some twenty-five or thirty gentlemen, appointed at a public meeting, in January of last year, to effect, if possible, this object, is still in existence. This Committee is evidently somewhat slow. No report of its proceedings has yet been published, and the only reason suggested for its silence is, that there has been nothing good to report: an insufficient reason.

But these gentlemen have not been entirely idle. It seems that immediately on their appointment, they called on the respective Presidents of the nineteen street railway companies, and, in a courteous manner, requested them to withdraw from their list of running regulations the rule excluding colored people. Some few favored compliance, more or less conditional, the others not; but all, or nearly all, finally settled on the subterfuge of referring the question to a carvote of their passengers. The subterfuge answered its purpose, for the self-respecting part of the community did not vote.

Shortly after this vote was taken, a colored man was ejected from a car by the help of a policeman. The Committee called on the late Mayor Henry, and respectfully inquired if this had been done by his order. His reply was: "Not by my order, but with my knowledge and approbation; as the right to exclude colored people has been claimed by the railway companies, and has not been judicially determined, the police assists in maintaining the rules of the companies, to prevent breaches of the peace." And he added: "I am not with you, gentlemen; I do not wish the ladies of my family to ride in the cars with colored people." It is proper to state here, that at the time of this interview, the latest three decisions of the Courts of the country, bearing on this question, had been directly against the right of exclusion — the last being that of Judge Allison, of our Court of Quarter Sessions.

The Committee then turned to the Legislature. A bill to prevent exclusion from the cars on account of race or color had been introduced into, and passed by the Senate, early in the session of 1865, and was referred to the Passenger Railway Committee of the House. Here it was smothered. No persuasion could in-

From Benjamin H. Hunt, *Why Colored People in Philadelphia Are Excluded from the Street Cars* (Philadelphia: Merrihew & Son, 1866), pp. 3–6, 16–19, 24–27.

duce this Railway Committee — twelve out of its fifteen members being Republicans, and eight, Republicans from Philadelphia — to report the bill to the House in any shape. According to the statement of the Chairman, Mr. Lee, the school-boy trick was resorted to of stealing it from his file, in order that it might be said that there was no such bill in the hands of the Committee. This assertion was made to an inquirer, several times over, by Mr. Freeborn, one of its members.

Finally, recourse was had to the Courts. Funds were raised, and within the last sixteen months, the Committee has attempted to bring suits for assault in seven different cases of ejection, all of which have been ignored by various grand juries — the last only a few days ago. In one case, a white man — a highly respectable physician — who interposed, by remonstrance only, to prevent the ejection of a colored man, was himself ejected. He brought an action for assault, and his complaint was ignored also. In five of these cases civil actions for damages have been commenced, which are still pending. One of them, by appeal from a verdict, given under a charge of Judge Thompson, in Nisi Prius, against the ejected plaintiff, is now on its way to the Supreme Court in banc, where it is hoped the whole question will be finally and justly settled.

The colored people at present rarely make any attempt to enter the cars. As is their wont, they submit peaceably to what they must. The last case of ejection was that of a young woman, so light of color that she was mistaken for white, and invited into a car of the Union Line by its conductor. When he found she was colored, he ejected her with violence, and somewhat to her personal injury.

Thus stands this matter at present; and such has been the action of official bodies in it. Let us now see what has been the action of the unofficial public, and what spirit that public has manifested towards it indirectly, by its action on kindred matters. The claim of the colored people to enter the cars, though a local question, is inseparable from the great policy of Equality before the Law, now offering itself to the national acceptance; and any local fact which bears on the one relates also to the other, and is therefore relevant to this subject.

And first, it is found that even colored women, when ejected from the cars with insult and violence, seldom meet with sympathy from the casual white passengers, of either sex, who are present, while the conductor often finds active partisans among them. But one white passenger has ever volunteered testimony in any case; and for want of this, generally the only proof possible, several cases have been dropped.

Events early last year, such as the voting in the cars, the petition of the men working at the Navy Yard for continued exclusion of colored people on the Second and Third Street Line, the "filibustering" of several hundred women, employed by the Government on army clothing, to defeat the Fifth and Sixth Street experiment of admission, and other acts of violence, show clearly that the classes represented by these men and women are bitterly opposed to admission.

Of our seven daily newspapers, two — the *Press* and *Bulletin* — have spoken out manfully and repeatedly in reproof of these outrages and in defence of the rights of the colored people. The others, it is believed, while admitting communications on both sides, have been editorially silent on the subject. In their local items, however, they have generally given a version of these disturbances unfavorable to the ejected colored people, under the heading of "riotous conduct of negroes," or some similar caption.

Grand juries, from the way in which their members are brought together, may be supposed fairly to represent the average public sentiment on this question, and their uniform action has been shown. Colored children have never been admitted to our general public schools, and the Associated Friends of the Freedmen in this city, who have lately adopted, as one of their cardinal rules, the admission of children of both colors, indiscriminately, to their schools in the South, consider that any effort to introduce the same rule here would be vain.

Only three members — Generals Owen, Tyndale, and Collis — of the Military Committee of Arrangements of sixteen, for the late celebration of the Fourth of July in this city, favored inviting colored troops to join in it; and the officers of the "California" Regiment (71st P.V.) gave notice, that if such troops did parade, their regiment must decline to do so, and would forward its colors to Harrisburg by express.

* * *

Aside then from the action of official and conventional bodies, it has been shown that large numbers of the laboring classes are opposed to the unreserved use of the cars by the colored people; and it must be inferred from the foregoing facts that but a small number of any class earnestly and actively advocate it. Between these extremes it is the great body of the respectable, intelligent and influential portion of the community, the members of which are generally self-restraining and above violence in speech or act, and who at first sight, one might suppose to be indifferent on the question, or perhaps torpidly in favor of admission. A little friction, however, brings to the surface unmistakable evidence that this body also is permeated with latent prejudice sufficient to carry it, imperceptibly perhaps and by dead weight only, but still to carry it against the colored people. Many belong to this class who would take offence if told so. It is not hard to find old hereditary abolitionists — Orthodox and other Friends, and members of the late Supervisory Committee for Recruiting Colored Regiments, who coldly decline all overtures for cooperation in this work. The abolition of Slavery away in the South was all very well, but here is a matter of personal contact. They are not opposed, themselves, to riding with colored people — certainly not. The colored people may get into the cars if they can; they will not hinder it. But they do wish there were baths furnished at the public expense, for the use of these friends, in order that they might be made thereby less offensive to ladies. And from these ladies, no doubt, comes an opposition — indirect and partially concealed — apparent perhaps only through the manner and tone of the father, husband or brother, but still most obstinate. It is often curious to observe how the discussion of this subject will set in motion two opposing moral currents in the same religious and cultivated female mind; that of conscience, which calls for the admission of the colored people, and that of prejudice, which hopes they will not get it. And thus the moral nature of many men and women, who in general are friendly to equal rights, on this question is divided. The sense of justice not being quickened by sympathy, their movements in respect to it are like those of a man palsied on one side — hindering rather than helpful. And it is this great, respectable and intelligent portion of the community that is really responsible for these wrongs and disturbances.

John Swift, a hard, shrewd man, now gone to his place, but in 1838 Mayor of this city, told a committee of Friends who called on him, on the 17th of May of that year, for protection against men who threatened violence, that "public opinion makes mobs;" and on the same night a mob, so made, after a short, mild speech from the said Mayor, counselling order and stating that the military would not be called out, burnt down Pennsylvania Hall. And every mob that the country has seen, during the last century, has had a similar origin and support, from that of the Paxton Boys against harmless Indians, in 1763, encouraged up to the threshold of murder, and then only opposed, when too late, by the Rev. Mr. Elder and his colleagues, to that of the New York Irish rioters against the negroes and the draft, in 1863, that was addressed as "my friends" by Gov. Seymour, the representative of a great party. And to bring this subject up to date, may be added the late rebel mob at New Orleans, hissed on, in its wholesale work of murder, by the President of the United States through the telegraph. The brain does not more surely impel or restrain the hand, than do the more educated and influential classes, however imperceptibly, those that are less so, in all cases in which premeditated violence is foreseen. And had there really existed any considerable degree of this moral restraining power in our community, these outrages against the people of color would long since have ceased.

We are forced then to the conclusion that this community, as a body, by long indulgence in the wicked habit of wronging and maltreating colored people, has become, like a moral lunatic, utterly powerless, by the exercise of its own will, to resist or control the propensity. And unless it finds an authoritative and sane

guardian and controller in the Supreme Court — unless this Court has itself, by chance, escaped this widely spread moral imbecility of vicious type, there seems to be no cure for the disease, nor end to its wickedness. And Philadelphia must still continue to stand, as she now does, alone, among all the cities of the old free States, in the exercise of this most infamous system of class persecution.

When Lear cries out "Let them anatomise Regan; see what breeds about her heart," we are made to perceive that his mind was not so wholly absorbed in his wrongs as to prevent it from speculating, in a wild way, on their cause: a touch of nature suggesting that any statement of wrongs which does not enter into the causes and conditions that made their commission possible, is imperfect. And to the question constantly recurring: What is it that has caused the people of Philadelphia thus to stand apart from other northern and western free cities, in the disposition to persecute negroes? the true answer seems to be this: Philadelphia once owned more slaves than any other northern city, with the possible exception of New York; she retains a greater number of colored people now, in proportion to her white population, than any other such city, with the accidental exception of New Bedford, when emancipation took place the process was left incomplete, and of all cities, north or south, she most fears amalgamation.

* * *

This fear greatly disturbs a large portion of our white population. In discussing the car question, an opponent of admission at once urges that it will be a stepping stone to amalgamation. The suggestion that seven disabled colored soldiers might safely be allowed equal privileges in a military hospital with 160 white soldiers, is put aside with the re-mark that such a rule would countenance amalgamation. The matron, with down-cast eyes and timid horror, intimates this objection to the reception, into the same Orphan Home, of little white and colored children, mostly between the ages of four and ten. All this sounds very illogical. Hitherto, there has been little amalgama-tion of the two races at the North, and as the colored people never make advances to the Whites, that little cannot be in-creased until the Whites make advances to them. When is this to begin? Let each one answer this question individually. This matter, in its negative aspect, rests entirely with the control of the white population.

The broad distinction, so often pointed out, between political and social equality, is still by many of our people persistently confounded, and perhaps it may be nec-essary to state it once more. Political equality everybody has the present or prospective right to demand — social equality nobody; for the barrier which separates the two is made up of private door-steps. Each of these, its owner has absolutely at his own command, and no man has a right to prescribe, even by implication, whom he shall permit, or forbid, to pass it. It is not an open question.

But supposing the relations, so long sustained at the North, between the two races, and which the Blacks do not com-plain of, when unaccompanied with wrongs, were suddenly to cease; and everywhere, North and South, on both sides, impelled by an irrepressible or-gasm, they should rush together. There are, in round numbers, 26,000,000 of white and 4,000,000 of colored people in the United States; and after every Black had found a White, there would remain 22,000,000 of Whites still unmated. These,

by necessity, would carry on the pure white population, and they might safely be left, without help, to sustain them-selves in the struggle of race, against the 8,000,000 of amalgamationists. But here it is asserted, they will receive aid from a distinct source. According to the theory of Doctors Nott and Cartwright, the mixed race rapidly decays, and after three generations dies out. This theory is accepted by those who fear amalgama-tion, and is often quoted by them, as an argument against the theory of equal rights. They also hate negroes and would be glad to see their numbers less. But pureblooded negroes, it is generally con-ceded, possess great vitality of race and are killed off with difficulty. This diffi-culty, it seems, can be overcome by amal-gamation. By this process, in one genera-tion, all these negroes become mulattoes, and this once accomplished, the whole African race is in a fair way to disappear from the land. These advocates for pure white blood have been defeating their own purpose. Let them reverse their policy and encourage, for a time, the amalgamation they have hitherto op-posed, and, with patience, they can have a white man's government yet.

This proposition is less extravagant than are these insane and wicked fears of impending amalgamation — wicked, because they are made the excuse, by the race that has the entire preventive control of the matter, for maltreating colored people and denying them rights which are accorded, without dispute, to every other man and woman in the country.

But these people will never come to such an end as this; and if it is true that amalgamation, here, leads towards it, then here, to any considerable extent, it will never take place. They were never made the valuable element of our popu-lation, which they are, simply to die out.

The greater part of the work which has yet been done on a large portion of this continent has been done by them, and apparently they ever will be, as they ever have been, absolutely essential to its full development.

This statement does not imply that the slave trade and slavery were right or necessary. The sin was not in the bringing of Africans to America, but in the manner of bringing them. God has established His own fixed laws to govern the movements of peoples, but He permits men to carry them out according to their will. Had men willed to be just and humane, they could have induced Africans to come to this continent as free emigrants; but they were selfish and wicked, and therefore forced them to come as slaves. Slavery has been, and is, destroying itself everywhere; and in this country, the great system of free labor and equal rights which prevails, without qualification, in some of the Northern States, is now being offered, and in spite of all opposition will soon be applied, to every State, north and south. It is not probable that it will stop there. It is believed that the same system is destined, in time, to be extended into our tropics. The so-called Anglo-Saxon race in England colonizes; in the United States it expands. Mr. Disraeli lately pronounced England more an Asiatic than a European power; and the day may come when we shall be as much a power of South America as we now are of North America. We have a means to facilitate future extension into the tropics in an element of our home population, suited to them, which England never possessed in hers; and after this has been received into our body politic, and is thus enabled to develop its powers, it is not easy to resist the conclusion that its destiny is to carry our civilization into these latitudes. The feeble and imperfect nationalities lying to the south of us are apparently but provisional. They are waiting a better system than their own, and higher powers than they possess, to apply it. The time is likely to come when their ability to furnish the products peculiar to their soil will fall short of the wants of the civilized world without; and should this be the case, it will stimulate us to carry thither our enterprise, and with it our laws and institutions. This has been the process by which they have been carried into California, by Whites alone — gold being the lure; but to places farther south our people of color, from their special climatic fitness for it, must assist in being their vehicle; and the two races must go towards the tropics, if at all, together. The African will never leave this country, but he may, in the legitimate pursuit of his own interests and happiness, assist in its expansion beyond its present limits; and, soon or late, should the practical assertion of our "Monroe Doctrine" make it necessary for us to carry our arms into tropical latitudes, the late war has shown us where to find soldiers. These are speculations, but it would be hard to show that they are without some groundwork of probable reality in the future. Meantime it is well to feel assured that these people are here for the good, and not the evil of both races, and that interest as well as justice demands that every right and privilege which we possess should be freely and at once extended to them. Let us trust God to do His own justice, not fearing that harm will come of it unless we interpose with our injustice; and let us no longer believe that if we do what is right and humane as a people to-day, we shall be punished for it tomorrow; for this is practical atheism.

IV. ETHNOCENTRISM AND RACE PREJUDICE

Robin M. Williams, Jr.: ETHNIC RELATIONS IN AMERICAN
COMMUNITIES

Disciplines other than history have applied themselves to the problem of searching out the sources of racial discrimination. Sociologists, psychologists, economists, anthropologists, and psychiatrists have investigated this phenomenon and rewarded scholars with a host of valuable insights. Illustrative of this fruitful labor is Robin Williams' masterful synthesis of what social scientists have said about ethnocentrism in American society. Professor Williams sees group membership, and hence ethnocentrism, as necessary to the psychological and material security of the individual. Thus, membership in one community generates attitudes toward significant outgroups. This need not be an unwholesome relationship, and indeed in a large, open, and pluralistic society such as ours, harmony requires that it must not be so. Still, ethnocentrism often does breed prejudiced attitudes and discriminatory behavior, including segregation.

In this selection, Professor Williams is concerned with the broad subject of intergroup relations in the United States. But his analysis can be applied to the study of Negro-white relations to reiterate points already made and introduce novel and important insights into the problem, present as well as past. First, it is obvious that white Americans can belong to many groups, but Negro Americans were and are relatively limited in such options. According to the principles which Williams advances, how has this affected the attitudes of Negroes toward their own racial group and toward those groups from which they have been excluded? Further, self-hatred and hatred of one's own group does occur, particularly where that group suffers prejudice and discrimination. Does it follow, then, that Negroes hate themselves and their society?

Positive ethnocentrism does not necessarily result in prejudice against other groups. On the contrary, harmonious relations between two groups seem probable when they enjoy a complementary economic relationship. Was this condition possible in either the Southern or the Northern economy in the 19th century? Is it possible in our modern industrial society? But if economic adjustment were possible in our past and present society, would not political, social, and sexual threats by both Negroes and whites still produce an acute crisis in race relations? It is also asserted that a closed belief system is a response to threat. Can you relate this to Cable's experience in the South in the

Robin M. Williams, Jr., *Strangers Next Door: Ethnic Relations in American Communities*, pp. 17, 19–26, 82–83, 139–41. © 1964. Reprinted by permission of Prentice-Hall, Inc., Englewood Cliffs, New Jersey.

1880's? What threat did Southern whites see in Reconstruction? What threat did Negroes see in Redemption? How did each manifest hostility? Do you see a "quieter prejudice" building in this postwar period as a result of "threat-hostility-threat?"

What is the role of understanding in Negro-white relations? Would racial harmony be promoted by a perfect understanding of the goals of the Negro revolution? Sociological studies indicate that it is not color which fixes prejudice upon both Northern and Southern Negroes, but the assumption that color represents basic differences in values. What would be the result if white Americans understood that Negroes share with them the same basic value system? Finally, would the elimination of economic distinctions between the two races contribute to this end? What part might education play in this effort?

In the realm of race relations, what are the relationships between the personality of the individual and the requirements of his group? For instance, do racial attitudes of individuals always predict behavior in interracial situations? In what sense might one say that prejudice is "normal"? How would Professor Williams answer our previous inquiry as to the relative intensity of anti-Negro feelings among upper-class whites as opposed to those of the lower class? How important is history in fixing racial attitudes and actions? Do actions fix attitudes or do attitudes fix actions? Does segregation promote discrimination or does discrimination promote segregation?

E THNOCENTRISM, says William Graham Sumner, is that ". . . view of things in which one's own group is the center of everything, and all others are scaled and rated with reference to it."[1] It is a fact that men classify their fellows in a variety of ways and react to others as members of social categories. What is the nature of these groups that men form? How do they form them, and why? What is the nature of ethnocentric feelings, and how strong are they? The answers to these questions will constitute the main part of this chapter. We will also consider, in the final pages of this chapter, whether ethnocentrism necessarily results in prejudice. . . .

Why we are ethnocentric

All individuals need group belongingness and group anchorage. Without

[1] *Folkways* (Boston: Ginn & Company, 1906), p. 13.

stable relationships to other persons, without some group ties, the individual becomes insecure, anxious, and uncertain of his identity. In order to receive the emotional support of the group (that is, the family group, the neighborhood or school peer group) the individual must heed the opinions of other group members. In the homogeneous family group he learns definite codes for behavior within the group and for behavior towards other groups. The child discovers very early that agreement with group opinions and codes is rewarding. He learns that the teachings of one's parents and close associates are helpful in getting what he wants and avoiding what he does not want. To the extent to which the child finds the instruction of elders and peers reliable for achieving rewarding results, he learns to give credence to their opinions. The child's need is great for relationships of trust that mediate reality to him. And through group attachments and loyalties he learns also of group antipathies and conflicts. He perceives groups, then, as social units in which he can expect security and love or danger and negative emotional experience.

Secure identity as a member of an ingroup is not a free good, contrary to some first appearances, but is only to be had at a price. Often one must have already established credentials of other group memberships and of personal qualities and achievements. Furthermore, maintenance of a clear, full, and secure identity within the ingroup requires conformity to group norms. More exactly, the price of one's group identity is responsible reciprocity with other members, a reciprocity defined by mutually accepted norms.

The overlapping of groups

Particularly in our complex society, most individuals are members of more than one group. The child, aware at first only of his membership in a kinship group, slowly becomes conscious of other memberships. Piaget reports that only at the age of ten to eleven were the children he studied capable of understanding that they could be members of both a locality and a nation, and of understanding what a nation is.[2] By adulthood then, the individual is aware of a plurality of group memberships that help him identify himself. The person is rare in urban America today who feels a clear and strong sense of identification with one and only one

grouping or segment of the community and nation. The typical individual is a member of many ingroups (groups of intimate belonging; "we-groups") and may relate himself to many other reference groups (those that matter to him, and upon whose opinions he relies).

It is difficult to realize fully the enormous significance of alternative group memberships. If the individual can belong to only one group, that group inevitably becomes all-important to him. In it all his satisfactions are found and are controlled and limited. It encompasses and constricts all his experiences. However, totalistic character of group membership diminishes in complex and fluid societies.[3] The growth of alternative possibilities of group membership and group reference depends upon the number and variety of distinctive groupings, but the sheer multiplication of groupings is far from the whole story. Changes in the criteria of membership are accentuated by changes in the functions of groups and by shifts in the alignments among and between groups. The characteristics that actually are statistically typical of a grouping or category at one time cease to be typical later.

A specific example of ethnocentrism

The following description of the upper-income, socially elite residents of Hometown will illustrate how similarities in occupation, income, background, ethnic origins, and style of life can cement a collection of individuals into a sociopsychological unity.[4]

[2] J. Piaget and Anne-Marie Weil, "The Development in Children of the Idea of the Homeland and of Relations with Other Countries," *International Social Science Bulletin*, III, No. 3 (Autumn, 1951), 561–78: ". . . the feeling and the very idea of the homeland are by no means the first or even early elements in the child's make-up, but are a relatively late development in the normal child, who does not appear to be drawn inevitably towards patriotic sociocentricity." (p. 562)

[3] Of course we recognize that multigroup societies can be engulfed by political totalitarianism, which enforces a new kind of all-encompassing membership.

[4] This description is based on Leila Calhoun Deasy's *Social Mobility in Northtown* (Unpublished Ph.D. thesis, Cornell University, 1953). Data were gathered from interviews with 126 women who clearly were members of the local upper stratum.

Among the socially elite of Hometown there is not a single Negro, Jewish, or Italian-American person. Members of the elite are native born of native-born parents. Most of them were born in Hometown, have inherited high social prestige, and form a self-chosen "village" within the city. Catholics are rare in the inner circles, although some Catholic adherents are found in peripheral circles. Elite members are overwhelmingly members of prestigeful Protestant churches and are Republicans in politics. Family background is a crucial factor in acceptance into the elite. The wrong ethnic background is automatically enough to insure exclusion. The elite grouping is difficult to enter and difficult to leave. Once in, a family is relinquished with reluctance, and much deviant behavior may be tolerated in the interests of group loyalty, exclusiveness, and protective secrecy against outsiders. Within the stratum most adults know, or know a great deal about, most of the others. And at least so far as the women are concerned, neither friendship, informal social participation, nor membership in clubs is sought outside these groups of like-circumstanced and mutually acquainted persons. . . .

ETHNOCENTRIC FEELINGS

Positive ethnocentrism

What are the components of the sentiments of ethnocentrism? George Peter Murdock says, "Always the 'we-group' and its codes are exalted, while 'other groups' and their ways are viewed with suspicion, hostility and contempt."[5] It is true that satisfaction with one's own group (Oog) sometimes is accompanied by negative feelings toward other groups, but for the moment let us examine the attitude that ethnocentric groups have toward themselves. The most important are:

1. A belief in the unique value of Oog.

2. Satisfaction with membership in Oog.
3. Solidarity, loyalty, or cooperation with regard to Oog.
4. Preference for association with members of Oog.
5. Belief in the rightness of Oog's relationships with other groups.

The attitudes toward other groups that often accompany the five sentiments just mentioned are:

1. Judging other groups by Oog's standards.
2. Belief that Oog is superior to other groups, in all ways or in some ways.
3. Ignorance of other groups.
4. Lack of interest in other groups.
5. Hostility towards other groups.

Negative ethnocentrism

It is not true, as is often assumed, that every group, people, or society considers itself superior in some generalized sense to all others or even to most others. There are many well-documented instances in which positive loyalty to the ingroup goes along with some appreciation of outgroup values and practices. One's own group does provide the norms for judging other groups, and in various particular ways an outgroup may be seen as superior. For instance, a tribe that prides itself upon its skill in the building of boats can recognize that the products of another tribe represent superior craftsmanship. This admission need not result in a general devaluation of Oog; it is negative ethnocentrism only in its admission of specific points of inferiority. One still retains one's ingroup standards and a basic adherence to its values.[6]

Yet, the phenomena of self-hatred and

---

[5] "Ethnocentrism," Encyclopedia of the Social Sciences, V, 613.

[6] Cf. Marc J. Swartz, "Negative Ethnocentrism," The Journal of Conflict Resolution, V, No. 1 (March, 1961), 75–81.

self-deprecation of one's own member-ship group are common and must be taken into account. History is replete with voluntary exiles, expatriates, out-group emulators, social climbers, rene-gades, and traitors. Also, the dominant attitude in a whole people can be one of accepting at least some of the low evalua-tions of outsiders. Peter A. Munch has given a fascinating account of such atti-tudes among the inhabitants of the re-mote island of Tristan da Cunha.[7] Among the villagers in southern Italy whose amoral familism has been described by Edward C. Banfield, the desire to emi-grate, the awareness of poverty, and the deprecation of the local society are evi-dent.[8] Other examples can be found, as in numerous instances of tribal peoples overwhelmed by conquest and subordi-nated to technologically advanced rulers. But the most important manifestations of negative sentiments toward the indi-vidual's own membership group occur in subordinated minority groups that are ob-jects of prejudice and discrimination. . . .

DOES POSITIVE ETHNOCENTRISM NECESSARILY RESULT IN PREJUDICE?

Whether strong negative feelings to-ward an outgroup always develop along with positive feelings of ethnocentrism is a question that has been explored in numerous studies. On the one hand we have Mary Ellen Goodman's study of Negro and white children, which showed that racial preferences were associated with hostility in only a minority of cases.[9] On the other hand, William Graham

Sumner is usually singled out among American sociologists as favoring the idea that ingroup solidarity is related to outgroup hostility. What he says, how-ever, is somewhat ambiguous: "The rela-tionship of comradeship and peace in the we-group and that of hostility and war toward others-groups are correlative to each other."[10] Sumner was thinking pri-marily of preliterate groups with rela-tively clear boundaries in situations in which threat and counterthreat affected the group as a whole. Even so, his state-ment bears the marks of caution: he says "are correlative" rather than "necessarily occur together.'" The consensus of studies, however, seems to be that continued interaction between culturally distinctive peoples need not result in conflict. One group may be assimilated by another, or there are even rare examples of sustained contacts between two endogamous and ethnocentric peoples with little conflict and little or no assimilation of one culture to the other.[11] Such accommodative rela-tions seem to rest upon an economic inter-dependence that is mutually advanta-geous and essentially noncompetitive. Much more common, unfortunately, are asymmetrical relations in which cultural differences become signals for discrim-inating behavior by members of a more powerful collectivity.[12]

Whether or not prejudice results is dependent on such complicated factors as 1) the nature of the social system of

[10] *Folkways*, p. 12.
[11] The case usually cited as an example has been described by E. J. Lindgren, "An Example of Culture Contact without Conflict," *American Anthropologist*, XV, No. 5 (October–December, 1938), 605–21. See also: John Gillin, "Race Re-lations without Conflict: A Guatemalan Town," *American Journal of Sociology*, LIII, No. 5 (March, 1948), 337–43.
[12] Cf. Hilda Kuper, *Indian People in Natal* (Pietermaritzburg: University of Natal Press, 1960).

[7] *Sociology of Tristan da Cunha* (Oslo, Norway: Det Norske Videnskaps-Akademi: I Kommisjon Hos Jacob Dywab, 1945).
[8] *The Moral Basis of a Backward Society* (New York: Free Press of Glencoe, Inc., 1958).
[9] Mary Ellen Goodman, *Race Awareness in Young Children* (Cambridge, Mass.: Addison-Wesley Publishing Company, Inc., 1952).

which the groups are a part, 2) the extent to which one group is a threat (economically or otherwise) to the other, and 3) the degree of understanding or misunderstanding of one group towards another. Other significant factors that will be discussed in subsequent chapters are the personality structures and dynamics of individuals within the groups.

The nature of the social system

When ethnic distinctions have been built into the cultural definitions and the norms of routine behavior in a social system, prejudiced attitudes and discriminatory behavior will be characteristic of normal personalities in that system. The manifestation of prejudice is not necessarily a symptom of unusual psychological needs or of neurotic or psychotic tendencies. When prejudice is normal in a society its manifestations are found among the respectable members of the population who are most firmly embedded in and committed to the legitimate organizations and conventional behavior characteristic of that social system. (Conversely, as shown by the findings in Southport, low prejudice is found most often among persons who are most likely to be free from the most constrained adherence to the general conventions of the community.) That is, when ethnic differences are the result of deeply rooted historical cleavages, it is usual for prejudice to accompany ethnocentrism.

Threat

If for any reason two clearly distinguished social categories or collectivities are so situated in a society that their members frequently come into competition, the likelihood is high that negative stereotyping (a common variety of prejudice) will reinforce a sense of difference and that hostile attitudes will tend to restrict interaction and/or cause conflict. Whether the competition is economic, political, sexual, or for prestige, if one group perceives another as a threat, prejudice results. A central implication of Rokeach's extensive résumé of research on dogmatism is that a closed belief system is a consequence of threat.[13] It is implied by this formulation that the greater the threat: (1) the more rigid the belief system that develops in response, (2) the more intense the affects supporting the belief, and (3) the more punitive the sanctions against disbelief.

Certain individuals and segments of the population will be so located in the social structure as to be especially likely to attach the meaning of threat, injury, deprivation, or punishment to the presence and behavior of one or more ethnic groups. Concretely, this most often means economic competition. For example, a white union member on strike sees "his" job taken by a Negro; a Protestant businessman believes his profits are reduced by the competition offered by a Jewish merchant. Or the so-called realistic threat may be noneconomic, such as when legislation thought to have been passed at the public behest of Catholic spokesmen confronts the Protestant with legal restrictions on dissemination of birth-control information or materials. . . .

When two ethnocentric groups come into a mutually threatening relationship, the stage for group conflict is fully set.[14] Short of the cycle of threat-hostility-threat that is the classical prelude to group conflict — from gang fights, to riots, to global wars — we can observe a quieter

[13] Milton Rokeach, *The Open and Closed Mind: Investigations into the Nature of Belief Systems and Personality Systems* (New York: Basic Books, Inc., 1960).
[14] H. M. Blalock, Jr., "A Power Analysis of Racial Discrimination," *Social Forces*, XXXIX, No. 1 (October, 1960), 58.

prejudice, stabilized in systems of preferential ranking and preferential social access and personal association.

Understanding and misunderstanding

The notion that understanding will always lead to the reduction of prejudice and/or the diminution of conflict has limitations that are often overlooked, ignored, or underestimated. Deadly enemies often understand one another all too well. Conversely, some groups manage to live together in a state of uneasy but tolerable accommodation when an accurate and detailed knowledge of each other's real sentiments and intentions would precipitate severe conflict. Understanding will reduce antipathy and the likelihood of conflict only if the groups like or respect what they discover by understanding each other or if one group finds that the threat posed by the other, though real, is not so severe, unalterable, or immediate as previously believed.

* * *

When persons feel themselves to be members of a group and identify themselves with that group's corporate views or policies in competition with another group, they necessarily find it difficult to comprehend the other group's position. An ingenious experiment by Blake and Manton[15] suggests that under these conditions a loss in competition leads to hostility both toward impartial judges and toward the winning group, ". . . with feelings expressed that the decision was completely unjustified in the light of the 'evidence.'" Even though the members of the competing groups reported that

they understood the competitor's views as well as they understood those of their own group, they, in fact, did not. In all groups, the members knew their own group's position best and were inclined toward distortion in their comprehension of the other group's position.

Misunderstanding another group's beliefs and values. Many observers, noting the relative unimportance of skin color biologically — and the failure of scientific studies to produce significant evidence of genetically determined racial differences in intelligence — have been puzzled to observe that many individuals persist in exhibiting prejudice towards those with physical racial characteristics. In studies done by Rokeach it has been revealed that prejudice may not be a result of the fact that the other person is of a different racial category, national origin, or religious group affiliation but a result of the prejudiced person's assuming that the other individual's beliefs and values are incongruent with his own.[16] He found that white students both in the North and in the South prefer a Negro with similar beliefs to a white person with different beliefs. But in most situations many white persons would take it for granted that the Negro person did differ from them in basic ways. Thus misunderstanding or lack of knowledge of the outgroup frequently results in prejudice.

Possibly one can now see why a wide range of concepts and types of data must be dealt with in order to begin to understand the causes and the nature of prejudice. Intergroup behavior involves three great systems of human social action: the culture, the social system, and the personality system. Accordingly, we need to study cultural content — "stereotypes," beliefs, and evaluations; and we need to

[15] Robert R. Blake and Jane Srygley Manton, "Comprehension of Own and of Outgroup Positions under Intergroup Competition," *Journal of Conflict Resolution,* V, No. 3 (September, 1961), 309.

[16] Rokeach, *The Open and Closed Mind.*

study personality as related to cultural content and to social interaction. We must analyze interaction both in terms of general patterns of intergroup contact and in terms of specific situations. And even while we deal with each of these sets of factors, we must remember that they all are simultaneously engaged in those person-to-person communications that are conceived by the participants to have an intergroup character.

Personality and prejudice

Prejudice a result of personality abnormality? In the process of socialization, the developing personality acquires a sensitivity to the values and expectancies of an ingroup and learns to differentiate between that ingroup and outgroups. If the ingroup is homogeneous and the larger culture supports stereotyped conceptions of certain social categories, then "prejudice" becomes a "normal" personality component. The fanatical bigot may be neurotic or psychotic, and his prejudice may be the vehicle for dealing with deep emotional disturbance — but so may hand-washing, anti-Red crusades, claustrophobia, *ad infinitum*. If there are neurotic and nonneurotic bigots, there are also neurotic and nonneurotic people who are tolerant. The prejudice of conformity is not necessarily the active prejudicial hostility of the true bigot.[17]

Consistency of personality. We know, further, that behavior in real situations is very imperfectly predictable from test responses such as the indorsement of verbal stereotypes in an interview. If human beings tend toward self-consistency, this would be manifested when they are asked about their opinions. Such testimony is typically highly organized.

But the consistency and continuity of personality are in part phenomena of values and concepts rather than of concrete behavior. Were this not so, behavior would be hopelessly rigid, for the "same" pattern of action has different meanings and carries different values in different situations.

The organized pattern of the personality may be impeccably clear and self-consistent. But we call it psychotic unless the person can accept the disturbances introduced by other personalities interacting with the individual in concrete situations. Unless paranoia is our model, we *expect* both behavioral variability and considerable looseness in the organizations of the personality as a system of values. For all these and other reasons, trait psychology is little help in this area, no more than in criminology where the net result of numerous studies is failure to demonstrate a consistent relation between specific traits and criminality.[18] The regularities that we call "personality" are not to be deduced from a fixed list of specific needs or predispositions.

Social responsiveness. Social action, then, is not simply an unfolding of personality traits. It is oriented to the reactions of others and their sensibilities, judgments, and feelings. Thus, social action is both more and less than the action that would follow from personality dispositions alone. It is *more* because it represents additional psychological elements and organizations of elements induced by orientation to the social object. It is *less* because some tendencies are not acted upon.

Men usually are to some degree socially

[17] Percy Black, "White-Negro Relations: A Different Slant," *Rural Sociology*, XIV, No. 3 (September, 1949), 261–62.

[18] Karl F. Schluessler and Donald R. Cressey, "Personality Characteristics of Criminals," *American Journal of Sociology*, LV (March, 1950), 476–84.

responsive. Indeed, the person who is completely impervious to the demands and expectations of others is regarded as possessed, insane, sick, or criminal, monstrous, and the like. Unless a person is responsive to the demands and expectations of *some* others, regardless of his momentary impulses and moods, he does not "perform his role" in the interrelations that constitute social life.

Thus we see that persons of different personality dispositions can be induced to act in similar ways, and persons of similar personality dispositions can be moved to act in different ways, by the presence and activity of others, or even by the remembered and anticipated judgments of others. To be sure, individuals differ greatly in extent and manner of social responsiveness (and responsibility). These differences are of very great importance. But the crucial fact remains that responsiveness is a basic normative requirement that is inculcated in children from earliest days in all societies and that is continuously demanded from other people. Personality needs and social requirements do not have to coincide exactly.

*   *   *

SEGREGATION, DISCRIMINATION, AND CONFLICT

Individual prejudices are not the explanation

The nature of change in the patterns of intergroup behavior also conflicts with the notion that individual prejudices completely account for discriminatory practices. If discriminatory behavior is based on personal prejudices, then the only way to change behavior is to eliminate prejudice. This is a slow process. Yet some forms of discrimination are abolished in a relatively short time. In May, 1954 the schools of Washington, D. C. were segregated; in September they were desegregated. The prejudices of Washingtonians were *not* so malleable, but the institutional pattern did change.

The inadequacies of individual prejudices as a means of predicting discriminatory behavior and accounting for changes in practices call for a reorientation in our thinking about these problems. A frame of reference is needed to explain the *variations* in discriminatory behavior as well as the *patterns* and to account for the persistence of some practices as well as the instability of others.

Changing and resistant patterns of discrimination

The kinds of discrimination that occur in American cities are not merely random or capricious. Although an integrated YMCA is sometimes found in a city where social mingling of the races is not considered to be appropriate, in more crucial areas of intergroup contacts the patterned nature of discrimination persists. There is a cultural component in the patterns of discrimination that resists change. The etiquette of race relations in some rural areas of the Deep South has changed little in the last fifty years.

The forms of prejudice and the patterns of discrimination are part of the cultural heritage. A generation ago, Bogardus found that white Americans objected to some nationality groups more than others.[19] Then, more recently he readministered the test and found that, in general, the order of rejection of the various minority groups remained the same. There are parallels in Negro-white relations. Whites often report that they would find it more objectionable to eat with a Negro than to work with a Negro,

[19] Summarized in G. E. Simpson, and J. M. Yinger, *Racial and Cultural Minorities* (New York: Harper & Row, Publishers, 1958).

and more objectionable to live next door to a Negro than to eat with him. The degree of personal intimacy has been suggested as the underlying dimension that explains the order of these items; however, this seems inadequate, since Negroes often live with whites as maids or nurses. Although the acceptance of Negroes in some situations and their rejection from others is difficult to explain, the effects are real. For instance, only 19 cities of the 248 in the nationwide sample permitted Negroes to get haircuts in white barbershops.

Cultural heritage prevails. Earlier it was suggested that individual prejudices do not solely determine whether or not a white person will participate in integrated activities with Negroes. Instead he tends to accept the prevailing practices of the situation in which he finds himself. The accepted policy regulating relations between the races in particular settings, then, becomes crucial. This policy can often be at variance with the local climate of opinion about race relations. For example, Southern ministers of both races may meet for lunch. Some institutional settings, such as a church or a union hall, regulated by policies of a strategic gate-keeper may be called segmental environments; these can either conform with or deviate from local opinion.

Deviations. Deviations from local patterns of discrimination are more likely to occur in some situations than in others. If the norms regulating interracial behavior are poorly defined in some situations, behavior in those situations is likely to be at variance with community sentiment. Where, for instance, do Negroes park their cars in drive-in theaters? The norms of some segmental environments may expressly forbid integration or insist upon it regardless of the prevailing community practices. The Masons, for instance, have a separate order for Negroes. On the other hand, Community Chest drives usually include both Negro and white workers. Finally, if there are competing sets of norms within any one organization, it may even happen that the tolerant set may prevail in intolerant communities, and the intolerant set may prevail in tolerant communities. There are integrated ministerial alliances in the Southern cities and segregated ones in the North.

The vicious circle of segregation

Without opportunities for getting to know Negroes, whites use the prevailing patterns of segregation and discrimination as a guide or model for their behavior in the few contacts they have with Negroes. Defensively, Negroes develop their own community life, which further reduces their contacts with whites, which in turn increases the possibility of misunderstanding and conflict, and so on in a familiar vicious circle.

Thus, we come full circle to the point at which we began this chapter. Restrictions and freedoms for intergroup contact and communication depend upon prevailing community definitions of what is appropriate and acceptable. These definitions emerge from shared social experience. Once interlocked into common expectations and interests, they set the boundaries for any given time, place, and situation for intergroup contact. But the experience of interaction, when it does occur, may in turn reinforce or modify the beliefs and norms that guide intergroup relations at the level where one man speaks to another.

Suggestions for Additional Reading

Until the pioneering labor was begun by Professors Woodward, Wharton, and Tindall, historians simply did not ask pointed questions about the nature of Negro-white relations between the closing of the Civil War and the early twentieth century. There are studies, however, which touch upon the subject and which the reader will find rewarding. Woodward's *Origins of the New South, 1877–1913* (Baton Rouge, 1951) provides a sweeping and rich description of the historical terrain upon which the battle for discrimination was fought. A special work that is highly useful and serves also as a model of the biographical form is *Tom Watson: Agrarian Rebel* (New York, 1938) by the same author. Francis B. Simkins in his *Pitchfork Ben Tillman* describes another agrarian rebel, one who was at the heart of the white supremacy movement in South Carolina. An interesting view of an urban progressive in race relations is provided by Dewey Grantham's *Hoke Smith and the Politics of the New South* (Baton Rouge, 1958). Recent and especially relevant to the Woodward thesis is Frenise A. Logan, *The Negro in North Carolina, 1876–1894* (Chapel Hill, 1964). This volume might be profitably read in conjunction with Dr. Helen G. Edmonds' *The Negro and Fusion Politics in North Carolina, 1894–1901* (Chapel Hill, 1951). A valuable attempt to relate race and politics in the South is in Paul Lewinson, *Race, Class, and Party: A History of Negro Suffrage and White Politics in the South* (New York, 1932). A broad view of the Southern political scene is V. O. Key's *Southern Politics in State and Nation* (New York, 1949).

There are a number of studies that display in close detail the pattern of discriminatory legislation which grew up in the South at the turn of the century. Several key books are: Gilbert T. Stephenson, *Race Distinctions in American Law* (New York, 1910); Franklin Johnson, *The Development of State Legislation Concerning the Free Negro* (New York, 1919); Charles S. Mangum, Jr., *The Legal Status of the Negro* (Chapel Hill, 1940); Charles S. Johnson, *Patterns of Negro Segregation* (New York, 1943); and Pauli Murray, *State Laws on Race and Color* (Cincinnati, 1951).

The concept of race which lay behind behavior in interracial situations is presented in Thomas F. Gossett, *Race: The History of an Idea in America* (Dallas, 1963). Guion G. Johnson focuses precisely upon this subject in the post-Reconstruction South in an article entitled "The Ideology of White Supremacy, 1876–1910," in *Essays in Southern History*, ed. Fletcher M. Green (Chapel Hill, 1949). An excellent survey of much of the literature which attempted to "codify" racial philosophy after the turn of the century is Idus A. Newby's *Jim Crow's Defense: Anti-Negro Thought in America, 1900–1930* (Baton Rouge, 1965). A recent argument that the Negro is inherently inferior is contained in *Race and Reason: A Yankee View* (Washington, 1961) by Carleton Putnam.

The testimony of contemporaries on the subject of race relations has a special value. One anti-Negro view was presented by Hinton Rowan Helper in *Nojoque: A Question for a Continent* (New York, 1867). Two liberal views are ably presented in George Washington Cable, *The Negro Question: A Selection of Writings on Civil Rights in the South* (New York, 1890), edited by Arlin Turner (New York, 1958); and Lewis H. Blair, *A Southern Prophecy: The Prosperity of the South Dependent Upon the Elevation of the Negro* (Richmond, 1889), edited by C. Vann Woodward (Boston, 1964). A broad range of protestations by Southern whites against the closing-out of the Negro from Southern society is well surveyed in Charles E. Wynes' *Forgotten Voices: Dissenting Southerners in an Age of Conformity* (Baton Rouge, 1967). The response of two Negro leaders to that movement can be seen in W. E. B. Du Bois, *The Souls of Black Folk: Essays and Sketches* (Chicago, 1903), recently edited by Saunders Redding (Greenwich, Connecticut, 1961); and Booker T. Washington, *Up From Slavery* (New York, 1902).

An interesting and, indeed, often exciting way to look at the history of any period is through novels, particularly those written by contemporary observers. A liberal attitude toward race relations in the Reconstruction period is evinced in *Bricks without Straw* (New York, 1880), a novel by "Carpetbagger" Albion W. Tourgée. A broader study of Reconstruction is contained in Tourgée's *A Fool's Errand,* first published in 1879 and recently reissued under the editorship of John Hope Franklin (Cambridge, 1961). An excellent study of the man himself is Professor Otto H. Olsen's *Carpetbagger's Crusade; the Life of Albion Winegar Tourgée* (Baltimore, 1965). The liberal view is advanced to the turn of the century by the first Negro novelist to gain a wide audience, Charles Waddell Chesnutt. His book, *The Marrow of Tradition* (Boston, 1901), is not only good history; it is also good literature. Novellike in its form, but a real and highly

readable story introduced by Lillian Smith is Ely Green's autobiography *Ely* (New York, 1966). The author of *Ely* was a mulatto boy who came of age about the turn of the century and is set in and about the university village of Sewanee, Tennessee.

The white supremacy point of view is presented in classic form in the work of Thomas Dixon. *The Leopard's Spots, a Romance of the White Man's Burden, 1865–1900* (New York, 1903) is perhaps the most appropriate novel for this purpose. Also useful is Dixon's *The Clansman; an Historical Romance of the Ku Klux Klan* (New York, 1905), the book which became the movie, *The Birth of a Nation* (1915).

There are several surveys of Negro history which the student will find valuable. John Hope Franklin's *From Slavery To Freedom: A History of American Negroes* (New York, 1947) is the best general treatment. Northern desertion of the Negro after Reconstruction is ably described in Rayford W. Logan's *The Negro in American Life and Thought: The Nadir, 1877–1901* (New York, 1954). An outstandingly perceptive study of a complex subject is August Meier, *Negro Thought in America, 1880–1915; Racial Ideologies in the Age of Booker T. Washington* (Ann Arbor, 1963); and an excellent vehicle for tracing that thought into current times is Francis L. Broderick and August Meier, *Negro Protest Thought in the Twentieth Century* (Indianapolis, 1966). The special and highly interesting history of "Black Nationalism" might be touched through E. David Cronon's biography of Marcus Garvey as *Black Moses* (Madison, 1955) and C. Eric Lincoln's *The Black Muslims in America* (Boston, 1961).

Sociologists have done much to enrich the literature of race relations in the

United States. A central topic is treated in Arthur F. Raper, *The Tragedy of Lynching* (Chapel Hill, 1933). A pioneering study of the sociology of the South is John Dollard, *Caste and Class in a Southern Town* (New Haven, 1937). Also interesting is the same author's study with Allison Davis, *Children of Bondage; the Personality Development of Negro Youth in the Urban South* (Washington, 1940). An insightful survey of interracial behavior in both slavery and freedom is Bertram W. Doyle's *The Etiquette of Race Relations in the South* (Chicago, 1937). The monumental study of Gunnar Myrdal has been mentioned previously: *An American Dilemma; The Negro Problem and Modern Democracy*, 2 vols. (New York, 1944). A sociological history is well presented in E. Franklin Frazier's *The Negro in the United States* (New York, 1949; rev. ed., 1957). Two very important recent works are Gordon W. Allport, *The Nature of Prejudice* (Cambridge, 1954), and

Thomas F. Pettigrew, *A Profile of the Negro American* (Princeton, 1964).

There is a rich store of readings available for the study of race relations in recent times. Most of this material is conveniently catalogued in Elizabeth W. Miller, *The Negro in America: A Bibliography* (Boston, 1966). If the student again chooses to use the novel as a tool to study the subject, there are many books to interest him. William Faulkner in *Light in August* (New York, 1932) and Lillian Smith in *Strange Fruit* (New York, 1944) are most rewarding. Negro novelists also often speak directly to the point, and they certainly speak with authority. Three views which survey the subject superbly are Richard Wright's *The Outsider*, Ralph Ellison's *Invisible Man*, and James Baldwin's *Go Tell It on the Mountain*. Not a novel but very interesting and informative is Pauli Murray's *Proud Shoes; the Story of an American Family*.

2345678910